Number 138
Summer 2013

New Directions for Evaluation

Paul R. Brandon
Editor-in-Chief

Mixed Methods and Credibility of Evidence in Evaluation

Donna M. Mertens
Sharlene Hesse-Biber
Editors

Mixed Methods and Credibility of Evidence in Evaluation
Donna M. Mertens, Sharlene Hesse-Biber (eds.)
New Directions for Evaluation, no. 138
Paul R. Brandon, Editor-in-Chief

Microfilm copies of issues and articles are available in 16mm and 35mm, as well as microfiche in 105mm, through University Microfilms Inc., 300 North Zeeb Road, Ann Arbor, MI 48106-1346.

New Directions for Evaluation is indexed in Education Research Complete (EBSCO Publishing), ERIC: Education Resources Information Center (CSC), Higher Education Abstracts (Claremont Graduate University), SCOPUS (Elsevier), Social Services Abstracts (ProQuest), Sociological Abstracts (ProQuest), and Worldwide Political Science Abstracts (ProQuest).

NEW DIRECTIONS FOR EVALUATION (ISSN 1097-6736, electronic ISSN 1534-875X) is part of The Jossey-Bass Education Series and is published quarterly by Wiley Subscription Services, Inc., A Wiley Company, at Jossey-Bass, One Montgomery Street, Suite 1200, San Francisco, CA 94104-4594.

SUBSCRIPTIONS for individuals cost $89 for U.S./Canada/Mexico; $113 international. For institutions, $313 U.S.; $353 Canada/Mexico; $387 international. Electronic only: $89 for individuals all regions; $313 for institutions all regions. Print and electronic: $98 for individuals in the U.S., Canada, and Mexico; $122 for individuals for the rest of the world; $363 for institutions in the U.S.; $403 for institutions in Canada and Mexico; $437 for institutions for the rest of the world.

EDITORIAL CORRESPONDENCE should be addressed to the Editor-in-Chief, Paul R. Brandon, University of Hawai'i at Mānoa, 1776 University Avenue, Castle Memorial Hall Rm 118, Honolulu, HI 96822-2463.

www.josseybass.com

Editorial Policy and Procedures

New Directions for Evaluation, a quarterly sourcebook, is an official publication of the American Evaluation Association. The journal publishes works on all aspects of evaluation, with an emphasis on presenting timely and thoughtful reflections on leading-edge issues of evaluation theory, practice, methods, the profession, and the organizational, cultural, and societal context within which evaluation occurs. Each issue of the journal is devoted to a single topic, with contributions solicited, organized, reviewed, and edited by one or more guest editors.

The editor-in-chief is seeking proposals for journal issues from around the globe about topics new to the journal (although topics discussed in the past can be revisited). A diversity of perspectives and creative bridges between evaluation and other disciplines, as well as chapters reporting original empirical research on evaluation, are encouraged. A wide range of topics and substantive domains is appropriate for publication, including evaluative endeavors other than program evaluation; however, the proposed topic must be of interest to a broad evaluation audience. For examples of the types of topics that have been successfully proposed, go to http://www.josseybass.com/WileyCDA/Section/id-155510.html.

Journal issues may take any of several forms. Typically they are presented as a series of related chapters, but they might also be presented as a debate; an account, with critique and commentary, of an exemplary evaluation; a feature-length article followed by brief critical commentaries; or perhaps another form proposed by guest editors.

Submitted proposals must follow the format found via the Association's website at http://www.eval.org/Publications/NDE.asp. Proposals are sent to members of the journal's Editorial Advisory Board and to relevant substantive experts for single-blind peer review. The process may result in acceptance, a recommendation to revise and resubmit, or rejection. The journal does not consider or publish unsolicited single manuscripts.

Before submitting proposals, all parties are asked to contact the editor-in-chief, who is committed to working constructively with potential guest editors to help them develop acceptable proposals. For additional information about the journal, see the "Statement of the Editor-in-Chief" in the Summer 2013 issue (No. 138).

Paul R. Brandon, Editor-in-Chief
University of Hawai'i at Mānoa
College of Education
1776 University Avenue
Castle Memorial Hall, Rm. 118
Honolulu, HI 96822–2463
e-mail: nde@eval.org

CONTENTS

EDITORS' NOTES

A
n old Italian proverb reads, "What's old is new, what's new is old" (Melfi, 2011). This quote characterizes the story of mixed methods in the evaluation community in that mixed methods have been used by evaluators for many years. Many evaluators intuitively came to the conclusion that evaluations on complex social programs could be enhanced by the use of multiple methods; hence the combination of both quantitative and qualitative data in the same study is nothing new. Attention to mixed methods in evaluation was apparent in the *New Directions for Evaluation* (NDE) edited by Jennifer Greene and Valerie Caracelli in 1997 (Greene & Caracelli, 1997). Since that time, attention to mixed methods has increased exponentially, as evidenced by the launch of the *Journal of Mixed Methods Research* in 2007, which had an initial impact factor of 2.219 and ranked fifth out of 83 journals in the social sciences, interdisciplinary category, according to the 2010 Journal Citation Reports by Thomson Reuters (2011). The American Evaluation Association (AEA) Topical Interest Group (TIG): Mixed Methods in Evaluation was founded in 2010 and quickly became one of the largest of AEA's TIGs. And, the *Sage Handbook of Mixed Methods in Social and Behavioral Research* (Tashakkori & Teddlie, 2010) is in its second edition.

Increasingly, policy makers and funders seek markers of credibility of evidence from evaluators. As the stakes for demonstrating credibility escalate, discussions of philosophical and methodological issues surrounding the politics of knowledge building become more important. Assisting the pursuit of "credible evidence" is the turn toward evidence-based practices— that rely primarily on quantitatively driven methods such as the randomized controlled trial (RCT) gold standard by which the credibility of evaluation findings are judged. Based on assumptions associated with the postpositivist paradigm, these tools help the evaluator to limit and measure the extent of bias in evaluation findings through a reliance on strict experimental design and measurement procedures. The evaluation community demonstrated its valuing of mixed methods in evaluation in its response to the U.S. Department of Education's (2003) decision to prioritize scientifically based evaluation methods. AEA responded with a statement praising the department for prioritizing evaluation of its programs, but also cautioned that limiting evaluators to a single, quantitatively focused approach would not be in the best interests of achieving the goals of improved educational experiences (AEA, 2003). AEA's official statement noted that the use of mixed methods, in a rigorous way, had the potential to address a

NEW DIRECTIONS FOR EVALUATION, no. 138, Summer 2013   © Wiley Periodicals, Inc., and the American Evaluation Association.   Published online in Wiley Online Library (wileyonlinelibrary.com) • DOI: 10.1002/ev.20052 broader number of issues as to how and why a program might be effective or not.

As interest in and attention to mixed methods grows in the evaluation community, it seems reasonable to ask about the connection between the call for evidence-based programs and the potential contribution of mixed methods to the creation of credible evidence. The purpose of this issue is to examine the contributions of mixed methods evaluation and its emerging philosophies, theories, and practices that can enhance the credibility of findings from RCTs, as well as opening up the possibility of enhancing credibility with evaluations that start from several paradigmatic stances, such as postpositivism, pragmatism, constructivism, and transformativism. The authors of this issue examine a range of truth claims with regard to mixed methods evaluation in general, and aim to examine critically the logical truth claims that surround the implementation of mixed methods evaluation designs.

The scope of this issue covers advances in mixed methods evaluation from philosophical, theoretical, and praxis perspectives. In the past, many higher-education evaluation programs prepared students in quantitative and/or qualitative methods; hence, many evaluators are self-taught about the topic of mixed methods. Herein, we offer frameworks and strategies for promoting rigor and for harnessing the synergy that the combination of two different methods can create, whereby one method can enable the other to be more effective and together, both methods can also serve to provide a fuller understanding of the evaluation focus. Toward this end, this issue provides evaluators with a range of important philosophical and theoretical approaches combined with practice-based mixed methods strategies. The authors address issues evaluators encounter when designing and implementing their mixed methods evaluations and suggest ways to address these issues to enhance the credibility of their evaluations. Hence, we provide the thinking of leaders in the field of mixed methods within the evaluation context as a way of furthering our understandings of how to enhance credibility of evidence through the use of mixed methods. The chapters in this issue draw from multiple disciplines, such as education, health care, youth services, and environmental issues.

Issue Overview

This issue identifies the types of synergistic outcomes a mixed methods evaluation design can harness by examining how deploying different methodological perspectives can enhance understanding of what credible mixed methods evaluation is. The authors analyze how the implementation of a mixed methods design can enhance understandings of issues of difference within a given evaluation design. They explore how mixed methods designs can also further issues of social justice and social transformation. A large part of this issue addresses the specific philosophical issues evaluators face in implementing a mixed methods design; therein lies a much deeper challenge—that of crossing paradigmatic divides.

After an introductory chapter, the next three chapters describe the philosophical territories associated with mixed methods. Hall writes about the use of a pragmatic paradigm to justify mixed methods use. Mertens's chapter focuses on the use of the transformative paradigm as a framing for mixed methods evaluations that explicitly address human rights and social-justice goals. The Johnson and Stefurak chapter describes a dialectical stance in mixed methods in which they argue that there is a value-added dimension by adhering to constructivist and post-positivist assumptions in qualitative and quantitative phases in a single evaluation, in ways that provide for conversations across the paradigms to bolster the credibility of the evidence produced by both methods. These philosophical chapters include implications for evaluation methods emanating from the philosophical stances discussed.

The next set of chapters shifts the focus to the design of evaluations from theoretical and practical perspectives and addresses methodological and methods challenges more explicitly. The Hesse-Biber chapter provides a bridge between philosophy and practice as she examines the potential for increasing the credibility of evidence in RCTs when a multimethodology and mixed methods framework is used in the design and interpretation phases of the study. White's chapter also addresses the use of mixed methods in RCT designs, but he does so from the position that the evaluation issue drives the method decisions. Hence, his view is that RCTs are best for impact evaluations and that these can be combined with qualitative data collection to answer process evaluation questions. Frost and Nolas contribute further to the methods used in mixed methods evaluations by examining how multiple methods are used for triangulation; they illustrate their approach through an example of an evaluation of a youth inclusion program. Collins and Onwuegbuzie continue the emphasis on increasing rigor in mixed methods evaluations by critically examining sampling strategies that contribute to enhanced quality and credibility, and provide multiple illustrations of different mixed methods sampling strategies.

Caracelli and Cooksy address the challenging concept of synthesizing across evaluation studies in order to get a broader picture of the evidence about an intervention with their critical examination of how quality is assessed in evaluation syntheses, taking into account the role of mixed methods in the synthesis strategy and in the determination of the quality of the individual studies. Jennifer C. Greene contributes the final chapter, in which she provides reflections on the issues raised in the preceding chapters, as well as raises questions for evaluators to consider in terms of how mixed methods can or cannot increase the credibility of their findings.

NEW DIRECTIONS FOR EVALUATION • DOI: 10.1002/ev

Acknowledgments

Putting together this special issue benefited from the wisdom and assistance of others along the way. We wish to thank Norman Denzin for encouraging a dialogue among diverse scholars in the qualitative, quantitative, and mixed methods communities. We also benefited greatly from the feedback we received in presenting our initial ideas at the International Congress of Qualitative Inquiry (ICQI) and the American Evaluation Association's annual meeting. We wish to thank all the authors for their visionary articles that tackle many thorny issues that are of utmost importance to the evaluation community. The *New Directions* editors, Sandra Mathison and Paul Brandon, along with anonymous reviewers, provided us with feedback that enhanced the quality of this issue. We also wish to thank our families who loved us and supported us throughout the process of preparing this issue.

References

American Evaluation Association (AEA). (2003). *Response to U.S. Department of Education.* Retrieved from http://www.eval.org/doestatement.htm
Greene, J. C., & Caracelli, V. J. (Eds.). (1997). *Advances in mixed method evaluation. New Directions for Evaluation, 74.*
Melfi, M. (2011). *Italy revisited: Folk sayings on aging.* Retrieved from http://www.italyrevisited.org
Tashakkori, A., & Teddlie, C. (Eds.). (2010). *Sage handbook of mixed methods in social & behavioral research* (2nd ed.). Thousand Oaks, CA: Sage.

Donna M. Mertens
Sharlene Hesse-Biber
Editors

DONNA M. MERTENS is a professor in the International Development Program at Gallaudet University and editor of the Journal of Mixed Methods Research.

SHARLENE HESSE-BIBER is professor of sociology at Boston College.

Mertens, D. M., & Hesse-Biber, S. (2013). Mixed methods and credibility of evidence in evaluation. In D. M. Mertens & S. Hesse-Biber (Eds.), *Mixed methods and credibility of evidence in evaluation. New Directions for Evaluation, 138,* 5–13.

1

Mixed Methods and Credibility of Evidence in Evaluation

Donna M. Mertens, Sharlene Hesse-Biber

Abstract

We argue for a view of credible evidence that is multidimensional in philosophical and methodological terms. We advocate for the importance of deepening the meaning of credible evaluation practice and findings by bringing multiple philosophical and theoretical lenses to the evaluation process as a basis for the use of mixed methods in evaluation, thus providing evaluators with strategies for garnering more complex and diverse perspectives on the creation of credible evidence. ©Wiley Periodicals, Inc., and the American Evaluation Association.

U nderstanding mixed methods approaches in evaluation involves understanding the philosophical stances, theoretical perspectives, and practical strategies that have emerged in the research and evaluation worlds associated with advances in mixed methods. In this chapter, we provide a broad picture of advances in mixed methods related to philosophy, theory, and practice in the evaluation context.

What Is Mixed Methods?

In general, evaluators who use mixed methods employ designs that use both quantitative and qualitative data collection and analysis techniques to answer a particular question or set of questions in evaluations. It is important to understand that mixed methods is not just about (mixing and combining) methods. The use of any given method or set of methods in an evaluation is also tightly linked to specific epistemologies, methodologies (theoretical perspectives), and axiological assumptions, as well as being connected to particular stakeholder perspectives (Giddings, 2006; Greene, 2007; Hesse-Biber, 2010; Smith, 1987).

More specifically, evaluation questions are grounded in a particular philosophical paradigm or standpoint regarding the nature of reality (ontology) and what can be known (epistemology). Methodology provides the theoretical perspective that links an evaluation problem with a particular method or methods. Methodologies—theoretical perspectives on social reality—flow from one's assumptions about reality: Is it knowable? Is there a single reality out there, waiting to be found? Is reality socially constructed, consisting of multiple realities?

Evaluators' philosophical assumptions, including those associated with methodology, lead evaluators to ask certain questions and prioritize what questions and issues are most relevant to the evaluation. Evaluation studies within and across disciplines can hold a range of different methodologies that frame their methods practices: those methodologies that hold up the importance of studying the "lived experience" of individuals (interpretative methodologies); those methodologies that privilege the importance of hypothesis testing and causality as the most important goal of social inquiry (positivist and postpositivist methodologies); those methodologies that stress issues of power and control and social justice (transformative, feminist, and critical methodologies).

We can think of methodology as both the theoretical and procedural link that brings epistemology and method together: defining the type of evaluation, how the evaluation process should proceed, what methods to select, and how they are employed to get at the evaluation problem. A methodology can be revised during the evaluation to the extent to which an evaluator's epistemological beliefs allow for revisions. In fact, mixed methods are often discovered as a result of modifying more conventional evaluation projects when traditional methods fail to get at the aspect of social life the evaluator is interested in (Hesse-Biber, 2010). Jennifer Greene captures well the distinction between method and methodology:

> Most . . . methodologies have preferences for particular methods, but methods gain meaning only from the methodologies that shape and guide their use. . . . An interview does not inherently respect the agency of individual human life; it only does so if guided by and implemented within a methodological framework that advances this stance. So, any discussions of mixing methods. . . . must be discussions of mixing methodologies, and thus of the complex epistemological and value-based issues that such an idea invokes. (Greene, 2002, p. 260)

Greene and her colleagues note that methods are tools and their practice requires the evaluator to be conscious of the methodological perspective(s) they employ within their evaluation project that demands "thoughtful mixed method planning," whereby there is reflexivity practiced with regard to one's methodological standpoint. Each evaluator should strive to "figure out one's stance on the 'paradigm issues' in mixed method enquiry" (Greene, Benjamin, & Goodyear, 2001, p. 30). Good mixed methods practice then demands "consciousness of this organizing framework and adherence to its guidance for enquiry practice . . ." (p. 30).

Synergy and Mixed Methods Evaluation Designs

Some of the most important problems and prospects of deploying mixed methods evaluation designs across the evaluation process involve issues of mixing paradigmatic approaches, as well as combining forms of data collection and analysis; tackling the issue of "when" and "how to" deploy mixed methods evaluation designs to achieve the synergistic promise of mixed methods to enhance the credibility of evaluation findings; and the range of opportunities for doing so within a mixed methods evaluation design and implementation.

Mixed methods approaches are often portrayed as synergistic, in that it is thought that by combining two different methods (i.e., quantitative and qualitative), one might create a synergistic evaluation project, whereby one method enables the other to be more effective and together both methods would provide a fuller understanding of the evaluation problem (Greene & Caracelli, 1997).

Yet the question remains as to just how such a synergistic promise of mixed methods can be harnessed by evaluators and just how doing so can enhance the credibility of an evaluation. Specifically, how does an evaluator assess whether adding another perspective and/or method to the evaluation study enhances credibility? It may in fact be the case that a monomethod design may be more advantageous and less costly. The importance of examining paradigmatic points of view reenvisions the concept of credible evidence as a highly complex concept that goes beyond the definition of getting it right. Evaluators have multiple pathways toward obtaining credible evidence. Depending upon where an evaluator stands (his/her given paradigmatic stance), the conceptualization of what credible evidence is also changes and becomes much more complex and nuanced. Its valence in terms of how important it is to the evaluation process also changes. For a positivist, evidence is in the form of one truth that is out there and thus the method to obtain this evidence as truth is the deployment of an RCT design that seeks to "control" for internal and extraneous factors that might bias the seeking out of truth. Subjective perspectives of what credible evidence is have a far different concept of truth and note that "evidence" is a not a singular and fixed entity. Instead truth is conceptualized as multiple and socially constructed and therefore the goal of evaluation is to unearth the range of subjective and often subjugated understandings of what is "truth" or "credible evidence" from the perspective/experience of the stakeholders. This is a concept of credibility that expands and complicates the possibilities of understanding the social world and in so doing expands the knowledge base of what is considered to be credible evidence.

The evaluation community stands at an important point in history in which the need for methodological and methods strategies with which to examine and achieve the range and diverse perspectives of credibility is of utmost importance. Innovations in the mixed methods field have the potential to move the field of evaluation toward a more inclusive, socially just process than is possible with a monomethod approach. This goal can be achieved by centering the importance of taking into account and being reflexive about what paradigmatic approaches we bring to an evaluation project and critically examining the ways of knowing that enhance the complexity of what it means to gather credible evidence.

Evaluation Paradigms and Mixed Methods

The interdisciplinary landscape of mixed-methods evaluation is rich and can accommodate a range of paradigmatic approaches to the evaluation process. Philosopher Thomas Kuhn (Kuhn, 1962) introduced the concept of "paradigm" to the scientific community by arguing that the practice of science is usually characterized by a particular paradigm, or way of thinking. He asserts that all knowledge is filtered through a paradigm or set of paradigms that are currently dominant within a particular discipline or field. A paradigm is a theoretically constructed worldview that provides the categories and concepts through and by which science and social science constructs and understands the world. A paradigm tells us what is there and what is not, what is to be taken seriously and what is not, what are data and what are not. Kuhn argues that there are no facts that are paradigm free or theory independent, because those that we regard as facts can differ according to the worldview or paradigm we live and work within. Kuhn points out that the reasons why one paradigm wins out over another are primarily political in nature—often it is irrational and subjective phenomena that affect the development of science. The paradigm that emerges victorious is the one that has the most converts—it need not have the greater explanatory power. There is, then, a *politics involved in knowledge-building* enterprise.

The field of mixed methods contains a range of competing epistemological, theoretical, and methodological paradigms that have been deployed by the mixed-methods community in general and by evaluators in particular. The authors in this Special Issue address a range of some of these epistemological and theoretical leanings that are especially relevant to evaluation and also spell out and engage with their foundational assumptions. Contained within any paradigmatic worldview are important philosophical assumptions an evaluator brings to an evaluation project— their specific view of reality (ontology); their theory of knowledge building (epistemology) that asks such questions as: How do we know what we know? This query covers inquiries such as: Who can be a knower? What can be known? How is knowledge constructed? Any evaluation process starts with a conscious and/or unconscious set of assumptions with regard to these metaphysical stances. For example, what a given evaluator knows or assumes to be true and what he/she wants to know as a result of the evaluation process is the basis of his or her epistemology. An evaluator's epistemological base, then, impacts every phase of the evaluation process including any subsequent theoretical (methodology) and methods choices.

A theory (methodology) can be broadly thought of as an explanation of the workings of the social world, or a segment of it, which reaches outside what is a known empirical reality. To varying degrees, and varying degrees of consciousness, evaluators apply theory during the evaluation process. Methodology and methods are intimately linked to one another, with methods serving as tools for gathering and analyzing the empirical world. Although epistemology deals with fundamental questions about knowledge, methodology refers to an evaluator's combining of theory and methods within the evaluation process.

Lincoln, Lynham, and Guba (2012, p. 100) have characterized and categorized five paradigmatic perspectives that they assert are umbrella terms to denote the range of paradigmatic approaches to knowledge building: *positivism* (contains realist and hard science approaches), *postpositivism* (they term as a modification of positivism), *critical theory* (such as feminism and race perspectives, the goals of which are to create change for women and other oppressed groups), *constructivism* (an interpretative approach that gets at subjective meanings), and *participatory/cooperative* (including postmodern approaches where knowledge is based on participative reality on transformation and lived experience with awareness of the importance of cocreation of meaning between evaluators and stakeholders). This categorization of paradigms also contains assumptions about ethical praxis and value choices. It is important to stress that this categorization into five paradigmatic stances allows the evaluator to compare and contrast a range of knowledge-building stances. The act of categorization itself is socially constructed and has aspects of what Kuhn notes as the "politics of knowledge building."

When Lincoln and Denzin were queried about the possible confusion of labeling a paradigm as critical theory et al. and participatory/cooperative, they responded as follows:

> With respect to the paradigm-theory distinction: For us, a paradigm is a metaphysics, an integrated philosophical statement which encompasses

positions on ontology (what we believe the nature of reality to be), epistemology (what we believe can be known about that reality . . . and the best ways for coming-to-know), and axiology (the role of values, aesthetics within any inquiry) . . . Paradigms are the overarching cosmological statements to which we subscribe when we engage in research [evaluation]. . .

Theories are statements, usually integrated statements, within paradigms that give us some model or format for thinking about a phenomenon . . . [T]heories and paradigms are commensurate; that is, they exhibit resonance, such that theories are nested within and under paradigms. Paradigms do not contain theories which violate the paradigms' cosmological assumptions, and theories do not grow from cosmological assumptions which do not support the theory. Thus, they are related, as "parent" and "child"; that is, paradigms and theories belong in ontological and epistemological and axiological "families." (Y. Lincoln & N. Denzin, personal communication, March 19, 2006)

Given this clarification of the relationship between paradigms and theories, the field of mixed methods seeks to remap and reshape the paradigmatic landscape, often to address the thorny paradigmatic issues involved in the mixing of methods and methodologies within a single evaluation project. The first is *dialectical pluralism*, which is envisioned to stand at the nexus of the constructivist and postpositivist paradigms (Greene & Hall, 2010; Johnson, 2010). Dialectical pluralism is seen as a philosophical stance that allows evaluators to engage in mixed methods inquiries while experiencing the tension between the assumptions of the postpositivist and constructivist paradigms. Another, the *pragmatic paradigm* (Biesta, 2010; Morgan, 2007; Johnson & Onwuegbuzie, 2004), supports the use of mixed methods based on the assumption that there is not one set of methods that is appropriate; rather, the criteria for choosing methods include what method fits with the evaluation questions. Biesta (2010), Greene and Hall (2010), and Denzin (2012) warn against an overly simplistic application of the pragmatic philosophy in evaluation, as in: If the method fits the question, then use it. Biesta (2010) outlines the basic principles of pragmatism as a philosophy that can inform mixed methods evaluators because Dewey held that no knowledge claim can be documented as providing the truth. Rather, different knowledge claims result from different ways of engaging with the social world. The *transformative paradigm* (Mertens, 2009; Mertens & Wilson, 2012) contains philosophical assumptions that emanate from an ethical stance that emphasizes the pursuit of social justice and the furtherance of human rights. Based on this axiological assumption, the evaluator is able to derive implications for the nature of reality, knowledge, and systematic inquiry that are commensurate with this ethical assumption. Hence, the nature of reality is looked upon as being multifaceted and reflective of different power positionalities in society. *Pluralist paradigms* (Frost & Nolas, 2013 [this issue]) stress the feasibility of conducting evaluation that traverses multiple methodologies and paradigms.

These paradigmatic stances have been deployed in the practice of mixed methods evaluation and also differ in how they approach the issue of incommensurability of paradigms when mixing methods. A pragmatic paradigm and pluralist paradigm, for example, directly provide strategies to combine paradigmatic approaches that are compatible with different sets of philosophical assumptions.

Although the use of mixed methods is not a required methodological decision within any of these paradigms, evaluators can align themselves with these paradigmatic stances and make decisions to use a single method because that is what is appropriate given the specific evaluation. In other words, paradigms do not dictate methods; rather, they guide thinking about methodological decisions. In undertaking the use of any methods (whether mixed or not), the evaluator needs to give consideration to the focus and the questions of the evaluation—what is it we want to know—and to be cognizant that all problems come from a perspective (transformative/feminist/critical, etc.). These perspectives in turn assume a given view of the social world and stance toward knowledge building (e.g., reality is out there and knowable; reality is multiple and subjective; etc.). Hence, evaluators who situate themselves within different paradigms will likely view the focus of the evaluation differently and will consequently ask different types of questions and make different methodological decisions.

Each of these paradigmatic approaches applied to mixed methods evaluation is also linked to specific types of methodologies (deploying a single or multiple set of methodological perspectives and evaluation questions) and in turn, these are linked to specific mixed methods practices/designs. Sometimes evaluators employ a single methodology and use mixed methods, for example, the postpositivist whose questions are in the service of this paradigmatic perspective, and who uses quantitative methods (as a primary method of inquiry) and deploys a qualitative method (to supplement primarily quantitative findings). This is not a dialectic stance but a monoparadigmatic mixed methods approach. Engaging two different paradigms means asking very different questions based on different views of the social world (e.g., positivism and constructivism). The methods chosen probably are in the service of answering different paradigmatic questions. This is illustrated by Greene's (2007) example of design as a dialectical stance whereby two philosophical frameworks are woven and in conversation so that each can be used to inform the other's approach.

Greene and Hall (2010, p. 124) describe a dialectic stance as follows: "A dialectic stance actively welcomes more than one paradigmatic tradition and mental model, along with more than one methodology and type of method, into the same inquiry space and engages them in respectful dialogue one with the other throughout the inquiry." This stance allows the evaluator to adhere to the beliefs of the postpositivist paradigm in conducting quantitative-oriented data collection and the constructivist in qualitative-oriented data collection and then to put the two in conversation with each other throughout the study to allow for deeper understandings based on the convergence and dissonance found in the approaches.

In conclusion, we argue that the use of paradigms as philosophical frameworks that delineate assumptions about ethics, reality, knowledge, and systematic inquiry helps to clarify the basis of disagreements among members of the mixed methods community. One paradigmatic position is not correct and the others wrong. However, continued debate about these frameworks provides fertile ground for expanding our understandings of the value and challenges associated with mixed methods evaluations.

References

Biesta, G. (2010). Pragmatism and the philosophical foundations of mixed methods research. In A. Tashakkori & C. Teddlie (Eds.), *Sage handbook of mixed methods in social research* (2nd ed., pp. 95–117). Thousand Oaks, CA: Sage.

Denzin, N. (2012). Triangulation 2.0. *Journal of Mixed Methods Research,* 6(2), 80–88.

Frost, N., & Nolas, S.-M. (2013). The contribution of pluralistic qualitative approaches to mixed methods evaluations. In D. M. Mertens & S. Hesse-Biber (Eds.), *Mixed methods and credibility of evidence in evaluation. New Directions for Evaluation, 138,* 75–84.

Giddings, L. S. (2006). Mixed-methods research: Positivism dressed in drag? *Journal of Research in Nursing, 11*(3), 195–203.

Greene, J. C. (2002). With a splash of soda, please: Towards active engagement with difference. *Evaluation 8*(2), 249–258.

Greene, J. C. (2007). *Mixed methods in social inquiry.* San Francisco, CA: Jossey-Bass.

Greene, J. C., Benjamin, L., & Goodyear, L. (2001). The merits of mixing methods in evaluation. *Evaluation 7*(1), 25–44.

Greene, J. C., & Caracelli, V. J. (Eds.). (1997). *Advances in mixed method evaluation. New Directions for Evaluation, 74.*

Greene, J., & Hall, J. (2010). Dialectics and pragmatism: Being of consequence. In A. Tashakkori & C. Teddlie (Eds.), *Sage handbook of mixed methods in social research* (2nd ed., pp. 119–143). Thousand Oaks, CA: Sage.

Guba, E., & Lincoln, Y. (1989). *Fourth paradigm evaluation.* Newbury Park, CA: Sage.

Hesse-Biber, S. (2010). *Mixed methods research: Merging theory with practice.* New York, NY: Guilford Press.

Johnson, B. (2010). A history of philosophical and theoretical issues for mixed methods research. In A. Tashakkori & C. Teddlie (Eds.), *Sage handbook of mixed methods in social research* (2nd ed., pp. 69–94). Thousand Oaks, CA: Sage.

Johnson, R. B., & Onwuegbuzie, A. (2004). Mixed methods research: A research paradigm whose time has come. *Educational Research, 33*(7), 14–26.

Kuhn, T. (1962). *The structure of scientific revolutions* (2nd ed.). Chicago, IL: University of Chicago Press.

Lincoln, Y. S., Lynham, S. A., & Guba, E. (2012). Paradigmatic controversies, contradictions, and emerging confluence. In N. Denzin & Y. S. Lincoln (Eds.), *The Sage handbook of qualitative research* (4th ed., pp. 97–128). Thousand Oaks, CA: Sage.

Mertens, D. M. (2009). *Transformative research and evaluation.* New York, NY: Guilford Press.

Mertens, D. M., & Wilson, A. (2012). *Program evaluation theory and practice.* New York, NY: Guilford.

Morgan, D. (2007). Paradigms lost and pragmatism regained: Methodological implications of combining qualitative and quantitative methods. *Journal of Mixed Methods Research, 1*(1), 48–76.

Smith, D. E. (1987). *The everyday world as problematic: A feminist sociology.* Boston, MA: Northeastern University Press.

Teddlie, C., & Tashakkori, A. (2009). *Foundations of mixed methods research.* Thousand Oaks, CA: Sage.

DONNA M. MERTENS *is a professor in the International Development Program at Gallaudet University and editor of the* Journal of Mixed Methods Research.

SHARLENE HESSE-BIBER *is professor of sociology at Boston College.*

NEW DIRECTIONS FOR EVALUATION • DOI: 10.1002/ev

Hall, J. N. (2013). Pragmatism, evidence, and mixed methods evaluation. In D. M. Mertens &
S. Hesse-Biber (Eds.), *Mixed methods and credibility of evidence in evaluation. New Directions for Evaluation, 138,* 15–26.

2

Pragmatism, Evidence, and Mixed Methods Evaluation

Jori N. Hall

Abstract

*Mixed methods evaluation has a long-standing history of enhancing the credi-
bility of evaluation findings. However, using mixed methods in a utilitarian way
implicitly emphasizes convenience over engaging with its philosophical underpinnings (Denscombe, 2008). Because of this, some mixed methods evaluators
and social science researchers have been criticized for an a-paradigmatic stance
(Greene, 2007). Critics posit that this seemingly unreflective "what-works"
(Denzin, 2012) approach threatens the validity of findings (Lipscomb, 2008).
This chapter maintains this position and argues that evaluators need to examine their philosophical orientations and how this informs credible evidence in
mixed methods evaluation. Accordingly, this work provides an overview of Deweyan pragmatism, emphasizing intelligent action. Next, important aspects of
intelligent action are used to explore central questions in mixed methods evaluation and evidenced-based practice. To conclude, a case example, illustrating
how intelligent action can inform mixed methods evaluation, is offered.*
© Wiley Periodicals, Inc., and the American Evaluation Association.

Scholars have expressed criticism when assessing the stance taken by
some mixed methods pragmatists. For example, Denzin (2012) argues
that mixed methods researchers misrepresent the philosophy of pragmatism when they promote a "what-works" approach. An example of this can
be found in Bryman's (2007) findings from interviews with mixed methods

U.K. social researchers. Findings revealed that "when asked about how far epistemological and ontological issues concerned them, most interviewees depicted themselves as pragmatists who felt it was necessary to put aside such issues to secure funding for their research interests and to publish their findings" (p. 17). In the case of these researchers, the "what-works" approach focused on doing what was efficient to advance their research agendas. Such findings suggest the current usage of the term *pragmatism* has been trivialized in the field of mixed methods, and that an a-paradigmatic (Greene, 2007) approach to mixed methods evaluation has emerged.

The most prominent example of the rise of an a-paradigmatic approach to mixed methods can be seen in the contemporary demand for credible evidence. Greene (2009) discusses how evidence-based evaluation is "not really about epistemology, defensible methodology, or warranted claims to know, even though framed as such. Instead, [it] represent[s] political principles and tactics to attain them" (p. 156). The privileging of randomized controlled trails could be considered such a tactic because it is considered the gold standard for providing the secure or credible knowledge needed to make decisions (Donaldson, Christie, & Mark, 2009; Schwandt, 2009). Greene's analysis is part of a highly complex and contentious debate about evaluation practice and the use of mixed methods to determine how evidence is generated and what makes it credible (Teddlie & Tashakkori, 2003).

However, Denscombe (2008) warns, "there is a danger" when a "what-works" or an a-paradigmatic approach is used in mixed-methods evaluation (p. 274). These approaches replace reflective mixed methods practice with expediency (Denscombe); lead to a methods-centric focus, which "can damage the credibility of research design, implementation and reporting" of mixed methods (Lipscomb, 2008, p. 33); provide limited "strategies for assessing the interpretive, contextual level of experience where meaning is created"; and eschew issues of ethics and social justice (Denzin, 2012, p. 83). Moreover, mixed methods, as described by Creswell and Plano Clark (2007), include philosophical assumptions that guide such things as data collection and analysis. This definition of mixed methods demands a link between philosophical ideas and methodology to direct decisions about what questions to ask, data interpretation, and the credibility of evidence (Lipscomb). There are some scholars who demonstrate how the pragmatic paradigm can be linked to mixed methods (see Feilzer, 2010); however, more examples are needed. Accordingly, this chapter examines pragmatism, focusing on how its philosophy can address questions about credible evidence, and enhance the praxis of mixed methods evaluation.

To begin, it is important to note that pragmatism is a diverse philosophical tradition, with contributions from classical pragmatists (i.e., Charles Peirce and William James) and neopragmatists (i.e., Richard Rorty and Cornel West). Rather than conflate these perspectives into one philosophy, this chapter focuses on Deweyan pragmatism, in particular, his thoughts on intelligent action. Further, it should be stated that pragmatism is not the only philosophical paradigm that is compatible with mixed methods evaluation (see Maxwell, 2010; Johnson & Stefurak, this issue; Mertens, this issue; Mertens & Wilson, 2012); nor is mixed methods "alone in its use of pragmatism as its philosophical underpinning" (Denscombe, 2008, p. 275). Yet Deweyan pragmatism is considered relevant to the discussion on credible mixed methods evaluation for the following reasons. First, the synergy between theory and practice in the "pragmatism embedded" in Dewey's work (Burke Johnson, personal communication, September 18, 2012) accomplishes contextual sensitivity and tangible processes for how inquiry and credible evidence are achieved. Second, his views on intelligent action advance reflection, ethics, and social justice. And third, Dewey's pragmatism is relevant because, like many evaluators, his main objective is to address societal problems by taking action in an intelligent way.

Deweyan Pragmatism

Dewey's philosophical roots are grounded in transactional realism, which moves away from the traditional dualism of objectivity and subjectivity (Biesta & Burbules, 2003). This perspective suggests that the mind and world are in constant interaction with each other through transactions. These transactions constitute an "adjustive process" (Biesta & Burbules, p. 10), whereby individuals actively engage, transform, or change the environment (Garrison, 1994). These transactional experiences also produce knowledge, which has the ability to reconstruct reality continuously (Garrison). Taken together, these assumptions imply that knowledge is "at the very same time constructed and real" (Biesta, 2010, p. 111) .

From a transactional realist perspective, then, the environment is not fixed but in flux. This constant change presents situations that require adaptive behaviors from individuals, which is why Dewey argues inquiry is critical to manage this uncertainty. It is important to note that Dewey does not consider inquiry in service to establishing universal or absolute truths. Truth, like knowledge, is temporal and embedded in and generated through our experiential transactions. Truth is linked to action, and has to be tested continuously and substantiated. It is in this way transactional realism supports an experimental inquiry approach in which verification plays a significant role to determine future actions. However, the central aim of Deweyan pragmatism is to move beyond mere experimentation to intelligent action.

Intelligent Action

Intelligent action begins with *problem identification.* Unfortunately, Dewey argues that problems are deemed problems because they have been accepted without question. When this happens, "the business of inquiry is but to ascertain the best method of solving them" (Dewey, 1938, p. 493). Rather than forgo examination, Dewey advances "analytic discrimination" to clarify the conditions, causes, and characteristics of a problem (Dewey, p. 493). However, the task of identifying the components of a problem, like truth, is never completely settled and continues throughout the evaluation process as new understandings come into focus.

Given the fluidity of problem identification, taking a "hypothetical" stance or mentally *considering various lines of action* becomes important (Campbell, 1995, p. 197). To do this, in addition to methodological approaches, diverse forms of information such as past and current directives, statutes, and historical data for addressing the problem must be considered. This also involves being aware of one's assumptions and taking the perspectives of others into account (Johnson & Onwuegbuzie, 2004). This creative hypothesizing can lead to a revision of ideas, an abandonment of ideas, or a selection of new ideas about which action to take (Biesta & Burbules, 2003). This imagining is also a form of *ethics*—a moral standard for conducting inquiry. Although imaginative thinking carries no guarantee for selecting the correct line of action, Dewey still thought this exercise ethically necessary to foster sympathy toward others' points of view.

Intelligent action also recognizes that inquiry takes place within communities of people, which represent dynamic entities with a "complex interaction of diverse perspectives" and experiences (Campbell, 1995, p. 184). Within these communities, communication becomes critical to coordinate the responses necessary to address problems (Biesta & Burbules, 2003; Johnson & Onwuegbuzie, 2004; Morgan, 2007). Communities represent a space for each person to reflect on his or her actions, the actions of others, and the consequences of those actions (Seigfried, 1996). Further, communities represent critical sites to promote the values of societal advancement (i.e., freedom, equality, and justice) or, to use Dewey's term, *democracy* (Campbell, 1995). Dewey's conception of democracy will be returned to later. First, a few thoughts on the outcomes of intelligent action are offered.

Inquiry outcomes, from a Deweyan perspective, are not viewed as definite solutions to the problem; they are viewed as *assertions* that become warranted in terms of their transferability in different situations (Johnson & Onwuegbuzie, 2004). This means that any assertions generated must be tested in real life; therefore assertions cannot be warranted until *after* actions have been taken. Transferability requires inquirers to work back and forth between the specific results and their general implications (Morgan, 2007). Moreover, Dewey argues that any knowledge gained or modifications made to our current knowledge based on warranted assertions should be shared in order to improve society—a goal of democracy.

Dewey's conception of democracy is different from a "political form of government"; rather, he considers democracy as a way of life (Middle Works 9:93, as cited in Campbell, 1995, p. 177). This broader view suggests democracy "must be continually explored afresh" in order to meet current needs and new circumstances (Later Works 11:182 as cited in Campbell, 1995, p. 177). Dewey's democratic commitment implies a world "in which we live and act together and for which we have a shared responsibility" (Biesta & Burbules, 2003, p. 108).

Intelligent Mixed Methods Evaluation and Evidence

With Dewey's philosophical roots in mind, the following sections offer the author's own conceptualization of how intelligent action informs mixed-methods evaluation with respect to the current demand for evidenced-based practice. Four questions central to mixed methods evaluation frame this discussion: What is being mixed? What counts as evidence? What makes evidence credible? And how can evidence be utilized?

What Is Being Mixed?

Within the discussion of mixed methods evaluation, the question of "what is being mixed in mixed methods" has a foundational role (Greene, 2007, p. xi). Mixed methods scholars suggest inquiry dimensions that are helpful for thinking about where the mixing occurs in a particular study such as mixing "philosophical paradigms" (Greene, 2007, p. 13). The transactional realism philosophy upon which pragmatism is based offers mixed methods an alternative epistemological platform. As such, the "historical philosophical incommensurabilities among paradigms are reconcilable" (Greene, 2007, p. 69). The point here is that Deweyan pragmatism does not perceive any "mixing" at the level of philosophical assumptions, because pragmatism itself is a philosophical perspective, thus making the question of philosophical compatibility irrelevant (Godfrey-Smith, 2003). Put differently, the pragmatist is critically concerned with the other dimensions of mixed-methods inquiry (i.e., theoretical assumptions, methodological traditions, data gathering, analysis techniques, personalized understandings, value commitments) (Greene, 2007).

When discussing feminist mixed methods, Hesse-Biber (2010) reminds evaluators "mixed methods are not inherently feminist"; rather, "they are tools or techniques researchers employ to answer specific research questions" (p. 170). Likewise, Deweyan pragmatism "embraces and promotes the mixing of methods" (Greene, 2007, p. 69), but within a particular perspective. Although Dewey's pragmatic perspective does not offer a *prescriptive* mixed methods approach or design per se, it does offer a *description* about how methods are to be considered. Pragmatically, mixed methods are used with the understanding that they are being utilized intelligently to attend to a specific problem, and to provide information that will help to make evaluative judgments. Typically, a qualitative methodological stance views the researcher as instrument (Mertens, 2010), whereas quantitative methods focus on instrumentation. Dewey's pragmatism invites evaluators to reflect critically on the instrumentation, the ways in which the evaluator is an instrument, and how the evaluation is instrumental in solving problems. Moreover, within the transactional framework, forms of mixing are conceptualized as ways to intervene in a situation. For effective intervention, strategies employed for mixing must have the capacity to change and adapt intelligently. Further, assertions generated from mixing will need to be revisited, and possibly revised after examination of their validity. Put succinctly, Deweyan pragmatism opens possibilities for different types of data, methods, and even assertions to be mixed based on the premise that both means *and* their consequences "are developed and perfected in the processes of continuous inquiry" (Dewey, 1938, p. 11).

What Counts as Evidence?

Within the context of evidenced-based inquiry, evidence is "narrowly interpreted to mean that only a specific kind of scientific finding—that is, evidence of causal efficacy—counts as evidence" (Schwandt, 2009, p. 199). Because Dewey's view on the inquiry outcomes does not refer to a specific kind of finding, this use of the term *evidence* is inadequate. This is why Dewey prefers the term *warranted assertion*. This term emphasizes "examinations of the relations which exist between means employed and conclusions attained as their consequence" (Dewey, 1938, p. 9). Warranted assertions are employed through a social process (think community) that utilizes "extensive prior knowledge" (think problem identification) for an "effective intellectual attack" (think use of appropriate methods, collaborative behaviors, and sympathetic attitudes) on the situation at hand (Dewey, 1938, p. 486).

What Makes Evidence Credible?

In evidenced-based practice, the credibility of findings centers on issues of methodological validity. Although this is important, Deweyan pragmatism adds a less-emphasized dimension to evidence-based practice: reflection. Reflection is the "active, persistent, and careful consideration of any belief or supposed form of knowledge in the light of grounds that support it, and the further conclusions to which it tends" (Dewey, 1910, p. 6). Dewey advocates that reflection be "employed as a method" in order to "grasp" beliefs, problems, and prior knowledge with "understanding"; thereby enabling them to take on "far-reaching significance they did not previously have" (Murphy, 1990, p. 68). Here we see how reflection also serves as a method to understand how problems can take on new meanings in relationship to the larger context within which they exist.

From analyzing multiple data sources, questioning assumptions, considering various lines of action, hypothesizing about consequences, to warranting assertions, reflective acts permeate Dewey's intelligent inquiry and form the basis of his "Principle of Credibility" (Murphy, 1990, p. 69). For Dewey, reflecting on inquiry practices *and* empirically testing assertions work to establish credibility. Thus, pragmatism advances a broad view of credibility, linking it to the processes *and* outcomes of evaluation.

Dewey's Principle of Credibility aligns well with Karen Kirkhart's conception of validity. According to Kirkhart (2005), validity is a multifaceted construct that is understood along the lines of methods, relationships, experiences, assumptions, and consequences. *Consequential validity* includes examinations of the consequences of understandings, judgments, and actions taken based on them (Kirkhart). Although Kirkhart and Dewey both recognize consequential validity, Dewey prioritizes this form of validity. Dewey (1923/1998) asserts, pragmatism "insists" upon consequences (p. 8). Pragmatism expands the role of credibility beyond examinations of methodological rigor to include continuous reflections on evaluation practices and the consequences they have in the lives of people.

How Can Evidence Be Utilized?

Utilization begins with the purpose of evaluation itself. Unfortunately, discussions focused solely on the use of evidence to establish causality misses this point (Biesta, 2010). In the case of Dewey, a main purpose of evaluation is democracy. This means that evaluation communities, institutions, and the like are purposeful to share information, take collaborative action, and promote social justice to meet human needs. Democracy from this perspective implies sympathy. Dewey reminds us that "wide sympathy, keen sensitiveness, persistence in the face of the disagreeable, balance of interests enabling us to undertake the work of analysis and decision intelligently are distinctly moral traits—the virtues or moral excellencies" (Dewey, 1920, p. 164). Sympathy is an explicit moral imperative that compels mixed-methods evaluators to reflect on how their evaluation addresses power dynamics and the interests of those least empowered. The democratic aims of pragmatism obligate the evaluator to utilize mixed methods in response to the cultural, political, and economic situations in our world so that these "situations are actually improved" (Seigfried, 1996, p. 262). Put succinctly, "social situations cannot be resolved pragmatically if such resolutions satisfy only those with the power to force a resolution or if it excludes those for whom the situation is problematic in the first place" (Seigfried, p. 263).

Putting Intelligent Action Into Practice

The chapter now turns to the use of Dewey's ideas in practice. A case study taken from an evaluation of a Leadership Academy is offered. The Academy was developed by a school district in a southeastern state in the United States to prepare aspiring principals.

The Leadership Academy: A Case Example

This exploratory mixed methods evaluation focused on participants' experiences in the Academy, and was intended to provide feedback to the district on the Academy's effectiveness in preparing principals for the job. The aspiring principals who participated in this assessment were part of the first cohort to go through the Academy. They were interviewed once after completion of the program to gather perceptions about the curriculum.

A major component of the Academy was the mentoring program. Principals were assigned a mentor at the time of being appointed, so the second interview with principals included questions about experiences with their mentors. This was intentional, as the principals were vulnerable in the sense that mentoring was a crucial part of their transition into the principalship. Principals were also asked to complete a survey on their sense of preparedness and the quality of the support they received from the district. To gain a better understanding of the role mentoring played in the professional development of principals, district mentors were also interviewed about their roles.

Based on the epistemological pragmatic perspective emphasizing the connection between the context and one's experiences, the evaluators considered the extent to which the Academy functions within a larger societal context, the mentorship program is embedded in the hierarchal organizational cultural of the district, and the mentor component of the Academy is fundamentally relational and representative of the district's hierarchy. With these contextual considerations in mind, multiple meetings were conducted during the evaluation to assess the impact of the mixed-methods approach on the evaluand. During these meetings, the team spent a considerable amount of time helping each other understand the "instruments" being used in the evaluation, critiquing the decisions they made while in the field, and discussing the district's impressions of the team's work based on periodic check-ins with key district administrators. These meetings assisted with data analysis and interpretation of findings because each team member was able to discuss areas of convergence and divergence. From a pragmatic perspective, these meetings were sites where actions were hypothesized and collectively agreed upon (unforced) to critically monitor and resolve emerging issues—methodological or otherwise.

Pragmatically, this evaluation allowed mixing to occur among multiple dimensions: (a) a mix of perspectives from a diverse evaluation team based on their own mentoring experiences and methodological skills, (b) a mix of methods/questions: wanting to know how much principals relied on the mentors (quantitative) and the nature of interactions (qualitative), (c) a mix of participant perceptions within and between groups, and (d) a mixing or integration of assertions. For example, a key finding from the survey was that principals perceived the mentor relationship to be effective, particularly in terms of showing respect and demonstrations of personal care.

NEW DIRECTIONS FOR EVALUATION • DOI: 10.1002/ev

The in-depth interviews contributed a better understanding of how personal care was concretely demonstrated because principals consistently described how much they appreciated the ability to call their mentors at any time. Interviews with the mentors corroborated the perceived effectiveness of the mentoring program, and also contributed to the identification of specific program activities that were highly instrumental in assisting novice principals (i.e., regular meeting times, and "just-in-time" training—when principals are actually doing the work).

The evaluation team crafted a report, which was submitted to the district with the understanding that more investigation about the effectiveness of the mentoring program is necessary. Accordingly, the team made plans to warrant their assertions as part of their evolving work with the district in this area (see Dirani, Freeman, & Skidmore, in press, for more detailed discussion of the mentoring component of the Academy).

This case example illustrates intelligent actions taken by these mixed methods evaluators, such as sympathetic understandings of stakeholders' perspectives, and critical reflections on the quality and consequences of their work as the evaluation unfolded. Each aspect of the project built iteratively on the next and so was part of a generative process.

Conclusion

This chapter has argued, in agreement with other scholars, that the philosophy of pragmatism has been misrepresented by some mixed methods pragmatists, making the point that the meaning of pragmatism has been trivialized to doing what is expedient or an a-paradigmatic stance. Mixed methods, by definition, demands a philosophical component to direct inquiry decisions (Creswell & Plano Clark, 2007). To address the misrepresentation of pragmatism, and to provide a philosophical companion to mixed-methods evaluation, a description and illustration of Deweyan pragmatism were offered. A closer look at Dewey's pragmatism reveals how "basing an argument for mixed methods on this version of pragmatism" may not be "misplaced," but perhaps serve to enhance the questions and praxis of mixed methods evaluation (Denzin, 2012, p. 82). It is true that Deweyan pragmatism "does not require a particular method or methods mix" (Feilzer, 2010, p. 14). The epistemological premise of Deweyan pragmatism would forego making a priori justifications for a specific mixed methods design, as this would be a fixed assumption. Rather, Dewey (1920) challenges such assumptions, and asks evaluators to "discover the meaning of the idea" by asking "for its consequences" (p. 163). Yet, as noted previously, Deweyan pragmatism does provide an alternative paradigm that promotes using mixed methods evaluation to solve problems by taking intelligent action.

Dewey's view on intelligent action serves to broaden the narrow focus on methodological rigor in evidence-based evaluation to include other validity constructs, yet, at the same time it prioritizes consequential validity. In contrast to traditional validity, which seeks an objective truth, consequential validity is primarily concerned with warranting assertions, requiring evaluators to work abductively, assessing the implications of their findings in concrete situations. This continual, contextually responsive approach enhances the credibility of mixed methods evaluation from a Deweyan perspective because it requires reflection—a lacking dimension in evidence-based evaluation. Reflection demands that evaluators imagine the implications their findings have on others. This requires ethical concern or sympathy. Without reflection and sympathy, consequential validity cannot be pragmatically assessed.

Reflection also enables pragmatic evaluators to use mixed methods in the service of social justice. Here reflection is used to assess continuously the extent to which evaluative endeavors promote values of democracy. Pragmatists are committed to improving society by addressing power dynamics, and considering issues of equity. And so, a pragmatic evaluator must be responsive to the economic, cultural, and social characteristics of the context at hand. In alignment with this perspective, the illustrative case study highlighted some of the ways in which pragmatic evaluators can critically reflect on and enact responsive actions as part of their evaluative activities. The pragmatic evaluators used reflection as a way to consider stakeholders' positionalities critically, maintain methodological flexibility, and assess their evaluative decisions relative to the context.

Reflection, from a Deweyan pragmatic perspective, then, is a method not only to warrant assertions, but also to examine the purpose of evaluation activities, question previously held assumptions, gain understanding, and examine the democratic aims of evaluation. Reflection is interwoven throughout Dewey's intelligent action philosophy. By recognizing the importance of reflection in combination with the empirical testing of assertions, Deweyan philosophy provides evaluators with the capacity to "discover the meaning" of "ideas" and problems, enhance the credibility of mixed-methods designs, as well as assess the consequential validity of their evaluative work (Dewey, 1920, p. 163).

In short, Dewey's philosophy provides mixed methods evaluators with a strategy to respond to our uncertain world not with uncertainty, but with intelligent action that "makes foresight possible and secures intentional preparation for probable consequences" (Murphy, 1990, p. 72).

References

Biesta, G. (2010). Pragmatism and the philosophical foundations of mixed methods research. In A. Tashakkori & C. Teddlie (Eds.), *Sage handbook of mixed methods in social and behavioral research* (2nd ed., pp. 95–118). Thousand Oaks, CA: Sage.

Biesta, G., & Burbules, N. (2003). *Pragmatism and educational research*. Lanham, MD: Rowman and Littlefield.

Bryman, A. (2007). Barriers to integrating quantitative and qualitative research. *Journal of Mixed Methods Research, 1*(1), 1–18.

Campbell, J. (1995). *Understanding John Dewey: Nature and cooperative intelligence.* Chicago, IL: Open Court.

Creswell, J., & Plano Clark, V. (2007). *Designing and conducting mixed methods research.* Thousand Oaks, CA: Sage.

Denscombe, M. (2008). Communities of practice: A research paradigm for the mixed methods approach. *Journal of Mixed Methods Research, 2*(3), 270–283.

Denzin, N. (2012). Triangulation 2.0. *Journal of Mixed Methods Research, 6*(2), 80–88.

Dewey, J. (1910). *How we think.* Boston, MA: D.C. Heath.

Dewey, J. (1920). *Reconstruction in philosophy.* New York, NY: Henry Holt.

Dewey, J. (1938). *Logic: The theory of inquiry.* New York, NY: Henry Holt.

Dewey, J. (1998). The development of American pragmatism. In L. A. Hickman & T. M. Alexander (Eds.), *The essential Dewey: Vol. 1. Pragmatism, education, democracy* (pp. 3–13). Bloomington, IN: Indiana University Press. (Original work published 1923)

Dirani, K., Freeman, M., & Skidmore, M. (in press). *Exploring mentor–protégé dynamics for school principals.*

Donaldson, S., Christie, C., & Mark, M. (Eds.). (2009). *What counts as credible evidence in applied research and evaluation practice?* Los Angeles, CA: Sage.

Feilzer, M. (2010). Doing mixed methods research pragmatically: Implications for the rediscovery of pragmatism as a research paradigm. *Journal of Mixed Methods Research, 4*(6), 6–16.

Garrison, J. (1994). Realism, Deweyan pragmatism, and educational research. *Educational Researcher, 23*(1), 5–14.

Godfrey-Smith, P. (2003). *Theory and reality: An introduction to the philosophy of science.* Chicago, IL: The University of Chicago Press.

Greene, J. C. (2007). *Mixed methods in social inquiry.* San Francisco, CA: Wiley.

Greene, J. C. (2009). Evidence as "proof" and evidence as "inkling." In S. I. Donaldson, C. A. Christie, & M. M. Mark (Eds.), *What counts as credible evidence in applied research and evaluation practice?* (pp. 153–167). Thousand Oaks, CA: Sage.

Hesse-Biber, S. N. (2010). Feminist approaches to mixed methods. In A. Tashakkori & C. Teddlie (Eds.), *Handbook of mixed methods research* (2nd ed., pp. 169–192). Thousand Oaks, CA: Sage.

Johnson, B., & Onwuegbuzie, A. (2004). Mixed methods research: A research paradigm whose time has come. *Educational Researcher, 33*(7), 14–26.

Johnson, R. B., & Stefurak, T. (2013). Considering the evidence-and-credibility discussion in evaluation through the lens of dialectical pluralism. *New Directions for Evaluation, 138*, 37–48.

Kirkhart, K. E. (2005). Through a cultural lens: Reflections on validity and theory in evaluation. In S. Hood, R. K. Hopson, & H. T. Frierson (Eds.), *The role of culture and cultural context: A mandate for inclusion, the discovery of truth, and understanding in evaluative theory and practice* (pp. 21–39). Greenwich, CT: Information Age.

Lipscomb, M. (2008). Mixed method nursing studies: A critical realist critique. *Nursing Philosophy, 9*(1), 32–45.

Maxwell, J. A. (2010). Using numbers in qualitative research. *Qualitative Inquiry, 16*, 475–482.

Mertens, D. M. (2010). *Research and evaluation in education and psychology: Integrating diversity with quantitative, qualitative, and mixed methods* (3rd ed.). Thousand Oaks, CA: Sage.

Mertens, D. M. (2013). What does a transformative lens bring to credible evidence in mixed methods evaluations? *New Directions for Evaluation, 138*, 27–35.

Mertens, D. M., & Wilson, A.T. (2012). *Program evaluation theory and practice.* New York, NY: Guilford.

Morgan, D. L. (2007). Paradigms lost and pragmatism regained: Methodological implications of combining qualitative and quantitative methods. *Journal of Mixed Methods
Research, 1*(1), 48–76.

Murphy, J. P. (1990). *Pragmatism: From Peirce to Davidson.* Boulder, CO: Westview.

Onwuegbuzie, A. J., & Johnson, R. B. (2006). The validity issue in mixed research.
Research in the Schools, 13(1), 48–63.

Schwandt, T. A. (2009). Toward a practical theory of evidence for evaluation. In S. I.
Donaldson, C. A. Christie, & M. M. Mark (Eds.), *What counts as credible evidence in
applied research and contemporary evaluation practice* (pp. 197–212). Thousand Oaks,
CA: Sage.

Seigfried, C. (1996). *Pragmatism and feminism: Reweaving the social fabric.* Chicago, IL:
University of Chicago Press.

Teddlie, C., & Tashakkori, A. (2003). Major issues and controversies in the use of
mixed methods in the social and behavioral sciences. In A. Tashakkori & C. Teddlie
(Eds.), *Handbook of mixed methods in social and behavioral research* (pp. 3–50). Thousand Oaks, CA: Sage.

*JORI N. HALL is an assistant professor in the Department of Lifelong Education,
Administration, and Policy at the University of Georgia.*

NEW DIRECTIONS FOR EVALUATION • DOI: 10.1002/ev

3

What Does a Transformative Lens Bring to Credible Evidence in Mixed Methods Evaluations?

Donna M. Mertens

Abstract

Credibility in evaluation is a multifaceted concept that involves consideration of diverse stakeholders' perspectives and purposes. The use of a transformative lens is proposed as a means to bringing issues of social justice and human rights to the foreground in decisions about methodology, credibility of evidence, and use of evaluation findings. ©Wiley Periodicals, Inc., and the American Evaluation Association.

C riteria for credible evidence typically revolve around specific types of designs, such as internal and external validity when conducting experimental designs and response rates in survey designs. As a broader look at the issue of credible evidence, this chapter explores the contributions made by adopting a transformative lens to inform the overall evaluation process. The transformative lens emanates from a paradigmatic stance that prioritizes issues of social justice and human rights as overarching ethical principles that need to permeate all aspects of an evaluation study. The principles that are associated with the transformative paradigm have emerged from inclusion of concerns raised by members of marginalized communities, such as feminists, racial/ethnic minorities, indigenous peoples, people with disabilities, and the deaf community. The implications of principles related to cultural responsiveness, reciprocity, resilience, and protection of community members are discussed in terms of how these principles improve the credibility of evidence that results from mixed methods studies.

The transformative paradigm pulls together many evaluation approaches that focus on issues of power and on addressing inequities in the name of furthering human rights and social justice (Mertens & Wilson, 2012). Evaluation theorists who support the use of their discipline as a tool for addressing injustice build on the early work of Robert Stake (1974) and his responsive model of evaluation, which emphasizes the importance of context and relationships with the stakeholders. Stake shifted evaluation's focus from large statistical studies conducted (sometimes at a distance) to determine a program's effectiveness to evaluations that were responsive to the stakeholders' experiences, beliefs, and values. Greene (2006), House and Howe (1999), and Mertens (2009) shifted that focus further to consider issues of social justice as they are embedded in the different stakeholder groups and how those differences demanded changes in evaluators' approaches.

Transformative Paradigm

The transformative paradigm emerged partially because of dissatisfaction with the dominant paradigms and practices in evaluation and because of the limitations of evaluations associated with these paradigms "that were articulated by feminists, people of color, indigenous and postcolonial peoples, people with disabilities, members of the lesbian, gay, bisexual, transsexual, and queer communities, and others who have experienced discrimination and oppression, as well as other advocates for social justice" (Mertens, 2010, p. 22). As these voices became more visible in the evaluation community, professional organizations such as the American Evaluation Association (AEA) revised their standards of ethics and developed agendas to be more responsive to transformative issues.

The transformative paradigm is one philosophical framework that helps to organize thinking about how evaluation can serve the interests of social justice through the production of credible evidence that is responsive to the needs of marginalized communities. It provides a metaphysical umbrella to guide evaluators who work in communities that experience discrimination and oppression on whatever basis—gender, disability, immigrant status, race/ethnicity, sexual identification, or a multitude of other characteristics associated with less access to societal privileges.

The transformative paradigm builds on the early work of Guba and Lincoln (2005) in which they defined paradigms in the evaluation world as being composed of sets of philosophical assumptions, including the following:

1. The *axiological assumption* about the nature of ethics.
2. The *ontological assumption* about the nature of reality.

3. The *epistemological assumption* about the nature of knowledge and the relationships between the knower and that that would be known (i.e., the evaluator and the stakeholders).
4. The *methodological assumption* about the nature of systematic inquiry.

I use these paradigmatic components to describe the transformative paradigm and derive methodological implications for each that serve to enhance credibility of evaluation processes and findings in the next section of this chapter.

Transformative Axiological Assumption

The transformative axiological assumption is characterized as accepting that the primary purpose of evaluation is to promote human rights and further social justice. This assumption leads to the realization that in order to work toward those goals, an evaluator needs to be cognizant of the power and cultural differences in communities where they work. In order to produce credible evidence, evaluators must identify those cultural norms, beliefs, and practices that support human rights and social justice and those that sustain an oppressive status quo. The evaluator can engage with stakeholders by arranging culturally appropriate opportunities to address the norms, beliefs, and practices that support or conflict with the pursuit of social justice. They can ensure that all stakeholder groups, especially those from marginalized and less powerful groups, are invited and supported in appropriate ways so that their voices are included throughout the evaluation. Although evaluators need to be careful not to overpromise changes that will come from involvement in the program and evaluation, they also need to design their evaluation in ways that facilitate leaving the community better off than it was before the evaluator departs.

The credibility of evidence is affected by the design of evaluations that are informed by the transformative axiological assumption in that methods need to be selected that allow for the discovery of cultural norms, beliefs, and practices (usually through the use of qualitative methods) and that lead to decisions about how to invite and include stakeholders appropriately. For example, in an evaluation of an early-intervention program for parents with deaf and hard-of-hearing children, a national quantitative survey revealed that certain subgroups of parents were significantly less satisfied with the services that they received (Meadow-Orlans, Mertens, & Sass-Lehrer, 2002). The evaluation team then decided to explore the reasons for the dissatisfaction through phone interviews with group representatives, thus demonstrating the use of a sequential mixed-methods approach to enhance credibility of findings. This strategy worked well with majority-race/ethnicity and hearing parents. However, it was less successful with deaf parents and parents from minority ethnic/racial groups.

The evaluators had to be aware of the cultural norms, beliefs, and practices of these parents and approach them in ways that were responsive to their needs. Deaf parents who do not use voice obviously cannot be interviewed through standard phone-interview strategies. Initially, the deaf parents were reached using TDD (Telephone Digital Device) that allowed the evaluators to type their questions and the participant to type responses back. However, the deaf parents felt that their experiences would not be accurately represented because typing in English is not their preferred mode of communication. They were afraid that they would appear to be inarticulate and exhibit low levels of literacy. They asked that we pay for interpreters that they chose to come to their homes in order that the deaf person could sign his or her responses, which would in turn be voiced by the interpreter into the phone. In this way, we were able to determine that their dissatisfaction with services was based on several factors, such as the poor signing skills of the service providers, lack of deaf role models for their children, and low expectations for their children because they are deaf. Such evidence can be used to support changes in preparation programs for early-childhood specialists so that they serve the needs of deaf parents and their children in more culturally appropriate ways.

For parents from minority racial/ethnic groups, we found that they experienced barriers to being available for phone interviews and they did not feel trusting of sharing their experiences with the evaluation team. Therefore, we went to programs that served a high percentage of parents from this group and asked the program directors if they would support us in collecting data from their parents. After checking with the parents themselves, the program directors told us that we could do focus groups on the site of the early-intervention programs. The use of focus groups was a qualitative strategy that contributed to our ability to capture the experiences of these parents accurately. These needed to be conducted at the time that the parents normally pick up their children at the end of the day, and we needed to provide child care, food, and transportation to support parents' participation. From this, we found some similar reasons for dissatisfaction, such as lack of appropriate role models and low expectations, but we also found reports of overt discrimination and patronizing attitudes of service providers. Again, the use of quantitative methods, followed by qualitative methods, designed with the transformative axiological assumption in mind, resulted in data useful for preparing early-intervention specialists in nuanced ways to respond to these subgroups of parents.

Transformative Ontological Assumptions

As illustrated in the previous section, people with different experiences have different perceptions of what is real. Is there one reality that we can know imperfectly? Or are there multiple realities; or are there different perceptions about what is real? Clearly, there are different opinions about what

NEW DIRECTIONS FOR EVALUATION • DOI: 10.1002/ev

is real and there are different consequences associated with accepting one version of reality over another. The transformative ontological assumption leads the evaluator to identify different versions of reality, interrogate their origins, and examine the consequences of accepting one version of reality over another. When the more powerful determine what is considered to be real in ways that oppress the less powerful, then the evaluator has a responsibility to reveal the dynamics of that situation.

For example, Katrina Bledsoe (2011) conducted an evaluation of an obesity reduction project in a high-poverty area with African American, Hispanic, and immigrant populations. The program designers assumed that the reason for the high rate of obesity in the school population was that the students had low self-esteem, so the researchers designed a program based on that version of reality. When Bledsoe asked the program developers if they had checked with the intended participants about their experiences with obesity, they indicated that they had not. Based on the transformative ontological assumption, she suggested that they needed to engage with diverse groups of students to determine their perceptions of the reasons that their weight was higher than was viewed as healthy, their motivations for wanting to reduce their weight, and strategies they might see as valuable in that regard. She combined the qualitative data from the students with quantitative data based on weight and blood work to develop a rationale for a different kind of program. This mixed methods approach revealed that the youth wanted to weigh less not because they had poor self-images, but because they were concerned about diseases associated with obesity such as diabetes and heart problems. They wanted to eat healthy foods, but they needed ideas for how to cook the foods they liked in healthier ways. The collection of qualitative and quantitative data in culturally appropriate ways at the beginning of the program changed understandings for the full range of stakeholders. By investigating these different versions of reality, the program developers were able to take a step back and revise the program so that it was more culturally responsive. The youth began to see potential for ownership in the program.

Transformative Epistemological Assumption

The transformative epistemological assumption concerns the relationship between the evaluator and stakeholders, as well as what is viewed as legitimate knowledge in the evaluation. Following from the transformative axiological and ontological assumptions, the epistemological assumption states that evaluators need to build relationships with stakeholders in culturally appropriate ways that acknowledge power differentials and support inclusion of all relevant voices, especially those who are traditionally marginalized.

Many members of marginalized communities are suspicious when evaluators arrive in their midst to study them, because they have experienced harm at the hands of researchers and evaluators and have been oppressed by the powerful majority who may have believed that they were doing what was best for these communities. For example, LaFrance and Nichols (2010, p. 14) state that "Evaluators—and their close friends, researchers—are not popular in Indian country. . . . The close connection between research and evaluation is problematic to many American Indian and Alaskan Natives whose tribes and families have suffered from a long history of intrusive studies that, while building the reputations of anthropologists and other researchers, have brought little to Indian communities and have actually resulted many times in cultural exploitation and the loss of intellectual property rights." Members of the American Sign Language community describe the harm that has come to them by the imposition of culturally inappropriate methodologies in the deaf community, which resulted in inaccurate and unflattering descriptions of deaf people (Harris, Holmes, & Mertens, 2009).

In accord with the transformative epistemological assumption, some communities are developing statements that define culturally appropriate interactions with them in research and evaluation contexts. For example, American Indians (LaFrance & Crazy Bull, 2009; Quigley, 2006), Maori (Cram, 2009), and Africans (Chilisa, 2012) developed ethical review boards that are rooted in their cultural traditions. Further, the American Indian Higher Education Consortium developed an indigenous framework for evaluation that emphasizes the need for respectful relationships amongst evaluators, stakeholders, and the land (LaFrance & Nichols, 2010). Terms of reference for conducting evaluations in the American Sign Language community emphasize the need for building respectful relationships, explicitly addressing issues of power by fostering interactive and empowering relationships in the form of coevaluators who are deaf and hearing and use of advisory boards that represent deaf and hard-of-hearing communities, and the right to expression in American Sign Language (Harris et al., 2009).

The American Evaluation Association's (AEA) Statement on Cultural Competency (American Evaluation Association [AEA], 2011) provides a bridge between the transformative epistemological assumption and the improvement of credibility of evaluations through the use of mixed methods. To support validity in evaluations, we are advised to "select and implement design options and measurement strategies in ways that are compatible with the cultural context of the study" (p. 5). This statement does not in and of itself necessitate the use of mixed methods. However, the use of appropriate mixed methods can be used to reflect diverse voices and perspectives accurately, in ways that reflect trustworthy understandings. For example, European-based evaluators of an HIV/AIDS reduction program in Botswana made assumptions about the cultural context in which a program was implemented that did not reflect the complexity of languages, power relationships between men and women, influences of poverty in the transmission of the disease, or the feeling of hopelessness experienced by some youth in that country (Chilisa, 2005). When Chilisa (2012) adopted a mixed methods, culturally appropriate design for the evaluation of an Afro-centric program to prevent HIV/AIDS infection for Botswana youth, she was able to integrate the qualitatively derived cultural understandings with the quantitative data on incidence of the disease to create a program that was effective. The change was not simply because mixed methods were used; rather, the change was the result of the application of a transformative lens brought to the design of a mixed methods study.

Transformative Methodological Assumption

Implications for the use of culturally appropriate mixed methods in pursuit of greater credibility of evaluations have been discussed for each transformative assumption in the previous sections. The transformative methodological assumption does not dictate the use of mixed methods; however, it does provide a rationale for the use of mixed methods as a way to capture the complexity of the phenomenon under study. Evaluators need qualitative assessment and dialogue time in the beginning of their planning in order to ascertain the cultural context in which they are working. Qualitative and quantitative data can be used together to facilitate responsiveness to different stakeholders and issues. The methods used need to capture the contextual complexity and be appropriate to the cultural groups in the evaluation. A cyclical design can be used to make use of interim findings throughout the evaluation study. And follow-up is needed to facilitate use to enhance the potential of the program-evaluation findings to achieve the strengthening of human rights (Mertens, 2009; Mertens & Wilson, 2012).

The American Sign Language community recognizes that there is no one methodology appropriate to conducting evaluations that meet their ethical terms of references. However, Harris et al. (2009, p. 111) state:

> Quantitative, qualitative, or mixed methods can be used; however, the inclusion of a qualitative dimension in methodology is critical in order to establish a dialogue between the researchers [evaluators] and the community members. Mixed-methods designs can be considered in order to address the community's information needs. However, the methodological decisions are made with a conscious awareness of contextual and historical factors, especially as they relate to discrimination and oppression. Thus, the formation of partnerships with researchers [evaluators] and the Sign Language communities is an important step in addressing methodological questions.

Bledsoe's (2011) work on an obesity reduction program in a high-poverty area in New Jersey provides an example of a transformative mixed methods design that increased the credibility of the evaluators for the full range of stakeholders. Bledsoe used mixed methods to gather data from the students through training youth as data collectors who could go to places and events where the students naturally congregated to interview them and also to collect quantitative data on the location of restaurants and fast-food outlets and availability of healthy foods at grocery stores or corner markets. The results revealed that the youth wanted to exercise, but preferred to do so through dancing. Thus, the mixed methods design included qualitative data used to identify the youth's worldview and quantitative data that provided a picture of the options for healthier eating and exercise in the community. These data were used to develop a program that included having food festivals in the community to demonstrate healthy ways to cook favorite foods and holding dances at the school with students wearing pedometers to compete for who took the most steps. In addition, biometric data were collected to indicate weight loss and overall health, students kept diaries about what they ate and when they exercised, and surveys were conducted with students and parents. The evaluation findings were discussed in community gatherings as a way of using the findings to increase their impact beyond the immediate student group participants.

Conclusions

The application of a transformative lens to evaluation does not always dictate the use of mixed methods. But mixed methods strategies allow for examining the cultural aspects that are essential for transformative work and allow for adaptation of data-collection methods to be culturally responsive and to integrate the demand for social action that is inherent in a transformative approach in the evaluation process. This supports the credibility of evidence from multiple perspectives and for multiple purposes.

References

American Evaluation Association (AEA). (2011). *Public statement on cultural competence in evaluation.* Fairhaven, MA: Author. Retrieved from http.www.eval.org

Bledsoe, K. (2011, November). *Transformative mixed methods.* Presentation at the annual meeting of the American Evaluation Association, Anaheim, CA.

Chilisa, B. (2005). Educational research with postcolonial Africa: A critique of HIV/AIDS research in Botswana. *International Journal of Qualitative Studies in Education, 18,* 659–684.

Chilisa, B. (2012). *Indigenous research methodologies.* Thousand Oaks, CA: Sage.

Cram, F. (2009). Maintaining indigenous voices. In D. M. Mertens & P. Ginsberg (Eds.), *Handbook of social research ethics* (pp. 308–322). Thousand Oaks, CA: Sage.

Greene, J. (2006). Evaluation, democracy and social change. In I. Shaw, J. C. Greene, & M. M. Mark (Eds.), *The Sage handbook of evaluation* (pp. 118–140). London, England: Sage.

Guba, E., & Lincoln, Y. S. (2005). Paradigmatic controversies, contradictions, and emerging confluences. In N. Denzin & Y. S. Lincoln (Eds.), *Sage handbook of qualitative research* (pp. 191–216). Thousand Oaks, CA: Sage.

Harris, R., Holmes, H., & Mertens, D. M. (2009). Research ethics in sign language communities. *Sign Language Studies, 9*(2), 104–131.

House, E., & Howe, K. R. (1999). *Values in evaluation and social research.* Thousand Oaks, CA: Sage.

LaFrance, J., & Nichols, R. (2010). Reframing evaluation: Defining an indigenous evaluation framework. *The Canadian Journal of Program Evaluation*, 23(2), 13–31.

LaFrance, J. L., & Crazy Bull, C. (2009). Researching ourselves back to life: Taking control of the research agenda in Indian country. In D. Mertens & P. Ginsberg (Eds.), *Handbook of social science research ethics* (pp. 135–149). Thousand Oaks, CA: SAGE.

Meadow-Orlans, K., Mertens, D. M., & Sass-Lehrer, M. (2002). *Parents and their deaf children*. Washington, DC: Gallaudet University Press.

Mertens, D. M. (2009). *Transformative research and evaluation*. New York, NY: Guilford.

Mertens, D. M. (2010). *Research and evaluation in education and psychology: Integrating diversity with quantitative, qualitative, and mixed methods* (3rd ed.). Thousand Oaks, CA: Sage.

Mertens, D. M., & Wilson, A. T. (2012). *Program evaluation theory and practice: A comprehensive guide*. New York: Guilford.

Quigley, D. (2006). A review of improved ethical practices in environmental and public health research: Case examples from native communities. *Health Education and Behavior*, 33, 130–147.

Stake, R. E. (1974). *Program evaluation, particularly responsive evaluation* (Occasional Paper No. 5.). Kalamazoo, MI: Western Michigan University Evaluation Center.

Donna M. Mertens is a professor in the International Development Program at Gallaudet University and editor of the Journal of Mixed Methods Research.

Johnson, R. B., & Stefurak, T. (2013). Considering the evidence-and-credibility discussion in evaluation through the lens of dialectical pluralism. In D. M. Mertens & S. Hesse-Biber (Eds.), *Mixed methods and credibility of evidence in evaluation. New Directions for Evaluation, 138,* 37–48.

4

Considering the Evidence-and-Credibility Discussion in Evaluation Through the Lens of Dialectical Pluralism

R. Burke Johnson, Tres Stefurak

Abstract

Credibility of evidence in evaluation is examined through the lens of dialectical pluralism (DP). Principles of procedural justice are a core element of DP and help justify outcomes of its application. A key message is that DP and the associated circle of scientific evidence and knowledge model can aid the evaluation community in producing an inclusive evaluation knowledge generation, dissemination, and use system, where practice-to-theory and theory-to-practice evidence continually inform each other in a multiple stakeholder environment. ©Wiley Periodicals, Inc., and the American Evaluation Association.

I n this article we first outline the characteristics of the process philosophy of *dialectical pluralism* (or more simply DP). Second, with the use of DP we "dialogue" with multiple literatures on evidence-based evaluation and knowledge. Then we construct an evaluation evidence and knowledge model based on the major issues identified in the literature. Last, we provide tentative answers to several questions about our version of "evidence-based evaluation" (EBE).

A Brief Overview of Dialectical Pluralism

DP is a *process* philosophy for dialoging with difference. It is a process philosophy because it is based on the assumption that much of reality is plural and dynamic rather than singular and static. It is also a process philosophy because it provides a process to consider multiple issues and perspectives interactively, even when they appear to be highly divergent and contradictory. There are three major characteristics of DP. First, we should dialectically listen, carefully and thoughtfully, to different paradigms/worldviews, disciplines, theories, and stakeholder and citizen perspectives. Second, we should explicitly ground each evaluation instantiation in our and our stakeholders' epistemological and social–political values to guide the project (including the valued means and purposes/ends) (cf. Fulford, 2011; Hall, Ahn, & Greene, 2012; Mertens, 2012). Because DP is a process, the specific combination of emphasized values and viewpoints to be packed into an evaluation can vary from project to project.

Third, although multiple kinds of justice are very important, *procedural justice* is at the core of DP. DP is based on a Rawlsian (Rawls, 2001) procedural justice model and Rawls's view of *reasonable pluralism.* Reasonable pluralism recognizes that multiple and very different views of "the good" are reasonable (e.g., different paradigms, value sets, religions), but, at the same time, users of a Rawls-inspired DP are encouraged to work together dynamically and collaboratively, building on each other's differences and strengths, and working for *justice as fairness* and *democratic equality.* Democratic equality requires equal liberties (Rawls's first principle of justice), but justice as fairness simultaneously tells us to work to improve the conditions of the least advantaged (a key part of Rawls's second principle of justice). The use of this kind of DP in evaluation should produce evaluative conclusions that are perceived and accepted as fair and justified (for the people involved and represented) because the stakeholders have agreed upon the *procedure.* This approach can be approximated in much evaluation practice.

Applied to evaluation practice, DP entails listening to multiple important stakeholders and working toward an evaluation that meets multiple (often divergent) needs, and includes multiple perspectives regarding the evaluand. Dialogue occurs among stakeholders (including program recipients), evaluators, and data sources. DP provides a process for collaboration and shared knowledge production that incorporates difference. At the group level, Johnson (2011) has provided many strategies to enable fruitful discussion of differences, including equal power, building trust, openness, honesty, constructive conflict, role taking, fractionation (i.e., breaking a contentious issue into smaller parts for initial agreement), building on small gains, tolerance, compromise, collaboration, and working toward win–win solutions. DP also can help one approximate some level of deliberative democracy in evaluation (cf. Davidsdottir & Lisi, 2007; Greene, 2000).

In evaluation, there is no categorical imperative or single rational rule for solving contentious issues, but DP provides a dialectical and dialogical *process* for gaining acceptance of process and likely acceptance of outcomes even if they are not in full agreement with the group's decision. In Scriven's "logic of evaluation," evaluators make values-based/embedded (i.e., "thick") claims, conclusions, and recommendations. Although these judgments are socially constructed, they are based on data and on justified process. Our "final" evaluative judgments are perhaps based on what Scriven calls *probative inference*, which is as good as we can do (but good enough!) in evaluation (Scriven, 2012). Probative inference is neither deductive nor inductive inference; it is inference to the best explanation and best judgment given agreed-upon ground rules and values and standards and data. One can argue that traditional empirical research also produces probative inferences that are thick as well as empirical. This is easy to see when one notes that social science research, like evaluation, has epistemological, social, and ethical values packed (often implicitly) into the inquiry process and judgments and outcomes.

Regarding values, the language used in the title of the well-known law/program "No Child Left Behind" implies that it is committed to epistemologically valued empirical outcomes (e.g., student success) and socially valued outcomes (e.g., equality and social justice for children with the least power and the most impoverished prior educational experiences). The federal program title (despite its operationalization and focus on testing during the Bush administration) indicates a program that is supposed to have socially valued "objective effects." We wish President Bush would have used DP, because it would have provided a way to engage the differences in values, approaches, and solutions to work toward the valued ends of *leaving no child behind* in one of the richest nations on earth (the United States). Because of its emphasis on values, DP is therefore also an ethical theory of democratic process.

In the next section we dialogue with some literatures relevant to evidence-based evaluation. The literatures are evidence-based evaluation, evidence-based practice, randomized clinical trials (RCTs) as best practice, practice-based evidence, and communities of practice. Each literature has its advocates, values, and data. In our review, we locate some key issues and values for consideration, and these will be incorporated into a knowledge model for evaluation later in this article.

Evidence-Based Practice and Its Critics

Evidence-based practice (EBP) is used extensively in the health sciences and generally follows a nomothetic science model where knowledge is viewed as universally/generally true. It also has the commonsense goal of making decisions and delivering programs based on the best available evidence (which is sometimes labeled best practices). According to Haynes,

Devereaux, and Guyatt (2002), EBP addresses three major issues: (a) objective needs of recipients, (b) preferences and values of recipients, and (c) best available evidence. Clinical expertise is viewed as the process by which practitioners collect data relevant to each of these issues and make decisions in their given situations. EBP is not, as often claimed, a sterile process of just doing what "scientific research and evaluations" say to do, but is a decision-making process that puts the clinician/evaluator/program administrator at the center and combines these three kinds of information to provide a service that is informed by science and, simultaneously, tailored to a given recipient's objective needs and subjective preferences. EBP includes collaboration between program/treatment providers and recipients.

EBP is part of a larger effort to bridge the gap between general program theory and scientific evidence and local practice (cf. Myers, 2008; Randall, 2002; Yorks, 2005). EBP emphasizes a top-down pipeline (Green, 2008) from program theory to local program administrators and practitioners. Following a natural science/postpositivist paradigm, EBP emphasizes the use of RCTs to test various interventions and treatments for human and social problems. RCTs use random assignment of participants to treatment conditions, standardized intervention protocols, a true no-treatment control group, specific inclusion and exclusion criteria to be labeled a "true experimental design," and a high degree of manipulation and control over extraneous variables. RCTs place high epistemological value on reducing biases, eliminating confounding/differential influence of variables, and maximizing internal validity. RCTs are criticized for not unpacking program/ treatment processes, not providing evidence of explanatory causation, and lacking understanding of subjective and intersubjective phenomena that are necessary for a full account of human-service outcomes (Hesse-Biber, 2012). The purpose of EBP (and RCTs) is to produce findings that allow strong conclusions about causal influences of programs and interventions— postpositivist "findings we can trust," and it is assumed that results will work generally and treatments need to be applied with fidelity.

The top-down-pipeline theory (or nomothetic-to-idiographic knowledge use) is somewhat reasonable in the context of biomedical interventions, where there is relative homogeneity of the target phenomenon. However, the logic weakens when we consider that most psychosocial and social phenomena are relatively heterogeneous and embedded in complex social contexts. The artificial settings in which RCTs are often conducted can yield results with poor external validity, and do not capture the dynamic interactions among client, provider, intervention, and context. RCTs can also be plagued by problems of low statistical power because of small sample sizes. RCTs should be *complemented* by more complex and locally embedded designs, including qualitative and mixed designs.

Beyond the limits of RCTs to capture complex and situational processes that govern phenomena, the top-down pipeline theory assumes program administrators and local practitioners can and will shape their behavior based on having consumed the scientific-evidence literature. There are concerns that such a pipeline does not exist, has never existed, and that even if it could exist, it would not provide a sound means of guiding local practice. McDonald and Viehbeck (2007) and others point out that the idea that practitioners learn to deliver services simply through analysis of data or acquisition of research findings flies in the face of what we know about how people learn. Practitioners often learn by having knowledge situated in a particular social context, not in an abstracted form. Our observations suggest that acquisition of evaluative/clinical/practical skills in human services and social programs occurs through social relationships in which training, mentoring, and supervision occur alongside consumption of nomothetic scientific findings. Thus, even if we could construct a program theory-to-practice pipeline, there is concern that it would not significantly improve the skills and outcomes of practitioners. A valuing of multiway dialogue (horizontally and vertically) is needed to link program theory to practice, and a values-engaged dialectical pluralism explicitly requires this process.

In human services, such as education and mental health, there are voices asserting that EBP is necessary to protect consumers from mere whims and intuitions of practitioners. Lillenfeld, Lynn, and Lohr (2002), writing in the field of clinical psychology, consider reliance on clinical expertise, experience, and intuition as a threat to the ability to deliver effective treatments. Gambrill (2010) laments that social work is based on the "authority" of the practitioner rather than guidelines derived from RCTs. We do not argue against the usefulness of RCTs, and we see their importance in establishing causation. However, we reject scientistic claims that only "scientific" knowledge is useful (Habermas, 1984; Miles, 2009).

Practice-Based Evidence and Its Critics

The term *practice-based evidence* originated in health care research, but has quickly expanded into other professions and disciplines. Practice-based evidence (PBE) involves using data gleaned from everyday practice and naturally occurring successes to draw conclusions about process and outcome and about varied and individualized ways phenomena operate (Horn, Gassaway, Pentz, & James, 2010). PBE flips the top-down pipeline on its head and uses participant observation of particular systems to produce knowledge (e.g., about idiographic and nonideal/unique contexts, situations, confluence of factors producing or inhibiting outcomes of interest). PBE is one corrective for balancing the still largely scientistic EBP model. PBE generally agrees with classical pragmatism's focus on continually adapting to and modifying our habits/practices/worlds to produce consequences we value.

Unfortunately, as practiced, PBE does not go far enough; it is not yet a bottom-up knowledge pipeline (where local/idiographic knowledge continually informs general/nomothetic knowledge). Increased funding and training for the local level and more frequent university–community collaboration can help with this. Increased use of grounded theory (and other qualitative methods) can help generate usable local knowledge.

Practice Research Networks and Communities of Practice

One form of PBE that appears to follow a dialectical pluralism principle of reciprocal knowledge at least minimally is practice research networks (PRN) (Audin et al., 2001). PRNs might have applicability in evaluation (and its reciprocal knowledge system) in that data are gathered from real-world service-delivery settings, often with large representative data sets, and the evidence is linked to an academic research entity. PRNs generate data from observational and qualitative studies of real-world service delivery and are continually fed the latest findings from academic-controlled settings. Pearce (2012) provides examples of multiple large federally funded studies that included ethnographic studies of subsamples. PRNs often include a multidisciplinary set of evaluation stakeholders and a values-based commitment to EBP models as well as collection of PBE (by evaluators and local program administrators) from real-world settings. The practice settings taking part in PRNs can help create contexts in which evaluation research activities become part-and-parcel of the culture of the service- and program-delivery setting. Unfortunately, as currently practiced in several program areas, PRNs often fail to understand fully and take into account practitioners' and clients' values and perspectives as emphasized by qualitative-research inquiry and DP.

One PRN model is the Society for Psychotherapy Research, which is a multidisciplinary organization of practitioners and researchers. British members of this group began a PRN in 1995 (Audin et al., 2001). This PRN is linked to the University of Leeds, which serves as a central clearinghouse for data and a coordinator of PRN meetings and activities. Data from protocols established for all participating entities are collected from psychotherapy clients in that setting and regularly forwarded to the university. Participants agree to use specific instrumentation to gauge outcomes for clients across multiple sites participating in both standardized/ benchmarked therapies, but also treatments that blend aspects of different therapies. The American Evaluation Association could advocate for similar PRN practices in evaluation.

McDonald and Viehbeck (2007) provide a similar concept based on the communities of practice (CoP) literature. Wenger's version (1998) includes the following key elements of CoPs: (a) mutual engagement, (b) joint enterprise, and (c) shared repertoire. The emphasis is on developing values, goals, methods, and targets of inquiry in a collaborative fashion involving multiple stakeholders. This model explicitly seeks to bring together stakeholders who would not otherwise interact and facilitate dialogue between knowledge producers and consumers/practitioners. The goal is not simply the production of outcome data but, first, the production of shared values and goals, which then guide the conduct of research. This practice provides an opportunity to produce knowledge that is "thick" with social values and is generated from specific contexts. It should please evaluators and program stakeholders operating locally and nationally. When contexts are well documented, program planners can make naturalistic generalizations (Stake & Trumbull, 1982) to determine if a particular research study should apply to their particular context.

McDonald and Viehbeck (2007) also document that the North American Quitline Consortium consists of researchers across the United States and Canada who seek to improve telephone-based smoking-cessation interventions. They conduct virtual seminars leveraging technology to enhance communication to share and disseminate their empirical findings and evaluative conclusions. The authors describe their own similar CoP project in Canada that targets smoking cessation that includes incentives for participation such as increased access to CoP resources. Both of these specific models seek to create a *culture of evaluation and practice* centered on a particular health-promotion problem and around which mutual construction of goals and methods of interacting and disseminating knowledge can occur. Another interesting CoP is the case of Xerox maintenance workers whose informal meetings created to share tricks of the trade ultimately became a formal company-sponsored CoP that disseminated practice guidelines across this multinational corporation (Brown & Duguid, 2000).

A Lingering Monism

As currently practiced, PBE and EBP are still rather entrenched in a postpositivist epistemology, and are, therefore, in need of greater dialogue with qualitative and mixed methods epistemologies and research practices. The current postpositivist leaning is not surprising, given the roots in health/medical research. In the next section, we suggest how to solve this problem by careful and thoughtful application of dialectical pluralism, which requires dialogue among epistemologies, value systems, paradigms, and methodologies. EBP claims to be concerned about local programs and people but it rarely incorporates phenomenological and ethnographic approaches to understand these people. PBE shares this interest, but it relies on objectivist methods. In short, we recommend future evaluation-based practice consider using mixed research driven by DP.

A Circle of Scientific Evidence and Knowledge Model

Figure 4.1 was developed based on our DP analysis of program theory and empirical findings. Our analysis suggests that evidence-based evaluation (EBE) should include national *and* local data and theory. The federal government and its funded projects hope to produce knowledge that works broadly.

Figure 4.1. Circle of Scientific Evidence and Knowledge Model

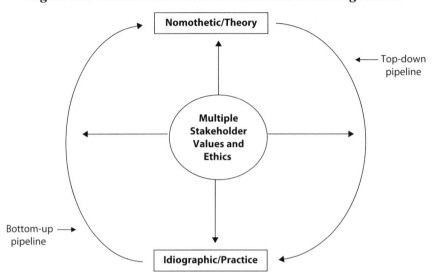

The national or federal perspective suggests the important arrow in Figure 4.1 is from the nomothetic/theory level of knowledge (i.e., theories/programs that work) down to the idiographic/practice/local level of knowledge; this is what was earlier called the top-down pipeline. However, local-level practitioners rarely rely on a single evaluation theory, and program administrators might not be aware of many of the principles of the program they are attempting to implement. Furthermore, these professionals have a *great deal of knowledge*. Evidence-based evaluation needs to learn local knowledge and inform evaluation and program theory. Qualitative methods can help obtain this extensive local knowledge (i.e., *local* strategies, models, and programs that work for specific people/groups situated in particular contexts). From this perspective, the important arrow in Figure 4.1 is from the idiographic/practice/local level of knowledge up to the nomothetic/theory level of knowledge; this is what was earlier called the bottom-up pipeline.

DP logic tells us to connect the top-down and bottom-up processes into a larger, *reciprocal* process. Theory should inform practice *and* practice should inform theory. When local professionals and practitioners are sufficiently knowledgeable, they will be able not just to adopt programs, but also adapt programs to local needs and contextual contingencies. Local knowledge about how a program works and how modified versions work should be fed into the reciprocal knowledge system shown in Figure 4.1.

Figure 4.1 also includes a values core. We will use Fulford's fitting label (2004, p. 207) and call Figure 4.1 a fact + value model. Embedding the system with epistemological, social, and psychological values is important because in the social and behavioral sciences and in evaluation, our knowledge is typically thick knowledge (the *is* and the *ought*, or the descriptive and normative, are merged in our outcomes and programs taken as wholes as they exist in the human world). Sometimes we forget that values are embedded in what we do, why we do it, how we do it, what we select to interpret, and what we produce. At the top level of evaluation operation in Figure 4.1, some common epistemically valued ends are reliability, generalizability, validity, prediction, explanation, justification/warrant, ameliorative, objectivity, correspondence, parsimony, and usability of the knowledge. Some common social values at this top level include beneficence, justice, utility, equality, integrity, and fidelity. At the lower/local level of evaluation operation in Figure 4.1, some common epistemically valued ends are discovery, intersubjective agreement, authentic knowledge, trustworthiness, contextual understanding, and applied knowledge that works in a specific real context with specific people. Some common social values at this bottom level include empowerment, freedom, happiness, justice, honesty, and health.

The reader can also see in Figure 4.1 the top-down and bottom-up ethics arrows. This is done to emphasize that epistemological and social and ethics-based values (a) embed the system and (b) should have downward and upward influences. DP tells us to understand, respect, share, and learn from others' values. From a practical standpoint, if a federal program conflicts with local values, a program is not likely to work. The downward ethics arrow suggests that broad ethical principles and theories will be important (e.g., utilitarianism, social-justice theory, soft versions of deontology). The upward ethics arrow suggests that we can and should learn from local ethics seen in cases, programs, and people, and that casuistry is one form of ethical theory that attempts to determine what is ethical in particular cases. DP tells us to listen and learn from multiple values and ethical principles and to determine the package that works best in each project/program instantiation.

We believe the dialectical/dialogical logic shown in Figure 4.1, when applied in evaluation, will foster continual improvement of evaluation knowledge (about our theories and evaluands), and, importantly, this knowledge will produce general and particular packages of values that we consider good. Over time, this *evaluation knowledge system* will "learn" more and more about our values and the complex interactions that are present in what we evaluate. Cronbach and Snow (1977) and Cronbach (1975) pointed this out many years ago. If we want practical theory, we have to accept that the world is complex and value embedded, and we will need to generate and use general and complex strategies and principles.

Some Questions and Tentative Answers for Evidence-Based Evaluation

Following are a few questions that we must deal with as evaluators in the new evidence-based world. After each question we provide a brief and preliminary answer based on our instantiation of the metatheory of DP.

- Is program evidence divided into two types: credible evidence versus the rest? The mixed perspective based on engagement of difference through the use of DP rejects binaries and single-reductionist-truth claims or monisms (one truth, one way to truth, one way of studying the world, one best method). Thus, the question provides a false choice. Better, the credibility of evidence should be viewed as a matter of degree and should rely on a package of evidence based on multiple continua. If it is to be valued, the evidence must have applicability locally. Evidence credibility should be high in evaluations using the process philosophy of DP because of its multiway dialogue and procedural justice used to construct the particular approaches and standards to be used for the evaluative claims.
- How should we approach the issue of a hierarchy of evidence (with RCTs placed at the top)? Use of DP leads us to realize that there is no single hierarchy of evidence because all kinds and instantiations of evidences have strengths and weaknesses. DP, our knowledge circle, and the basic principles of mixed research will help produce a holistic set of evidence.
- Is the experiment the only method we need to understand causation? General, *nomothetic causation* has been the goal of federally funded research, but we must also study complex and *idiographic causation* (nuanced, contextualized, and complex causation seen in local settings). Application of DP suggests that traditional quantitatively driven nomothetic research (searching for general laws that work in most places) is important, but of equal importance is idiographic causation (i.e., what qualitative researchers, practitioners, and historians of particular places and times and events provide) (van Noije & Wittebrood, 2010; Vogt & Johnson, 2011).
- Is only program adoption with fidelity important, or is program adaptation/modification in local contexts also a consideration? According to our application of DP, both are important and both should be part of the long-term goal of an evaluation knowledge system. Our system depicted in Figure 4.1 will help evaluators and their clients determine what works, where, when, and for whom by discovering (locally) *and* testing program theories (and adding contextual interaction terms), and sending "good" programs to new localities for further local testing, formative evaluation, and adaptation to local circumstances. This evaluation knowledge system will be in continual need of bottom-up–driven modifications, oftentimes resulting in contextual interactions in the general knowledge system.
- How can multiple social–political and epistemological values and standpoints be concurrently considered in the discussion over evidence? Through the use of a heterogeneous *team* of evaluators and stakeholders systematically packed with multiple social–political and epistemological viewpoints. Then, the team must engage in strategies gained from the conflict management and team-building literatures as well as Rawls's procedural theory of justice as outlined in the process philosophy of dialectical pluralism.

NEW DIRECTIONS FOR EVALUATION • DOI: 10.1002/ev

- How should evaluators warrant or justify their claims in a multiparadigmatic, multidisciplinary, multistandpoint, multistakeholder environment where some have much more power over the narrative of truth than others? This can be approached by inclusion of diversity in decision making and the use of team and procedural justice strategies. It is not perfect, but we should act where we are able. There are no panaceas, but dialectical pluralism can help.

References

Audin, K., Mellor-Clark, J., Barkham, M., Margison, F., McGrath, G., Lewis, S., . . . Parry, G. (2001). Practice research networks for effective psychological therapies. *Journal of Mental Health, 10*(3), 241–251.

Brown, J. S., & Duguid, P. (2000). Balancing act: How to capture knowledge without killing it. *Harvard Business Review, 78,* 73–80.

Cronbach, L. J. (1975). Beyond the two disciplines of scientific psychology. *American Psychologist, 30,* 116–127.

Cronbach, L. J., & Snow, R. E. (1977). *Aptitudes and instructional methods: A handbook for research on interactions.* New York, NY: Irvington.

Davidsdottir, S., & Lisi, P. (2007). Effects of deliberative democracy on school self-evaluation. *Evaluation, 13,* 371–386.

Fulford, K. W. M. (2004). Facts/values: Ten principles of values-based medicine. In J. Radden (Ed.), *The philosophy of psychiatry: A companion* (pp. 205–234). Oxford, England: Oxford University Press.

Fulford, K. W. M. (2011). The value of evidence and evidence of values: Bringing together values-based and evidence-based practice in policy and service development in mental health. *Journal of Evaluation in Clinical Practice, 17,* 976–987. doi: 10.1111/j.1365–2753.2011.01732.x

Gambrill, E. (2010). Evidence-informed practice: Antidote to propaganda in the helping professions? *Research in Social Work Practice, 20*(3), 302–320.

Green, L. W. (2008). Making research relevant: If it is an evidence-based practice, where's the practice-based evidence? *Family Practice, 15,* 20–24.

Greene, J. C. (2000). Challenges in practicing deliberative democratic evaluation. In K. E. Ryan & L. DeStefano (Eds.), *Evaluation as a democratic process: Promoting inclusion, dialogue, and deliberation. New Directions for Evaluation, 85,* 13–26.

Habermas, J. (1984). *The theory of communicative action, volume one: Reason and the rationalization of society.* Boston, MA: Beacon Press.

Hall, J. N., Ahn, J., & Greene, J. C. (2012). Values engagement in evaluation: Ideas, illustrations, and implications. *American Journal of Evaluation, 33,* 195–207.

Haynes, R. B., Devereaux, P. J., & Guyatt, G. H. (2002, March/April). Editorial: Clinical expertise in the era of evidence-based medicine and patient choice. *ACP Journal Club.*

Hesse-Biber, S. (2012). Weaving a multimethodology and mixed methods praxis into randomized control trials to enhance credibility. *Qualitative Inquiry, 18,* 876–889.

Horn, S. D., Gassaway, J., Pentz, L., & James, R. (2010). Practice-based evidence for clinical practice improvement: An alternative study design for evidence-based medicine. In E. J. S. Hovenga, S. Kidd, C. Hullin, & L. Cossio (Eds.), *Health informatics* (pp. 446–460). Washington, DC: IOS Press.

Johnson, R. B. (2011). *Dialectical pluralism: A metaparadigm to help us hear and "combine" our valued differences.* Presented in plenary session at the Seventh International Congress of Qualitative Inquiry, Urbana-Champaign, IL.

Lillenfeld, S. O., Lynn, S. J., & Lohr, J. M. (2002). *Science and pseudoscience in clinical psychology.* New York, NY: Guilford Press.

McDonald, P. W., & Viehbeck, S. (2007). From evidence-based practice making to practice-based evidence making: Creating communities of (research) and practice. *Health Promotion Practice, 8*(2), 140–144.

Mertens, D. M. (2012). Transformative mixed methods: Addressing inequities. *American Behavioral Scientist, 56,* 802–813.

Miles, A. (2009). On a medicine of the whole person: Away from scientistic reductionism and towards the embrace of the complex in clinical practice. *Journal of Evaluation in Clinical Practice, 15,* 941–949.

Myers, N. F. (2008). Bridging the theory-to-practice gap: Some thoughts from an internal OD consultant. *Human Resource Development Review, 7,* 469–471.

Pearce, L. D. (2012). Mixed methods inquiry in sociology. *American Behavioral Scientist, 56,* 829–848.

Randall, J. (2002). The practice–research relationship: A case of ambivalent attachment? *Journal of Social Work, 2*(1), 105–122.

Rawls, J. (2001). *Justice as fairness: A restatement.* Cambridge, MA: Belknap.

Scriven, M. (2012). The logic of valuing. *New Directions for Evaluation, 133,* 17–28. doi: 10.1002/ev.20003

Stake, R. E., & Trumbull, D. J. (1982). Naturalistic generalizations. *Review Journal of Philosophy and Social Science, 7,* 3–12.

van Noije, L., & Wittebrood, K. (2010). Fighting crime by fighting misconceptions and blind spots in policy theories: An evidence-based evaluation of interventions and assumed causal mechanisms. *American Journal of Evaluation, 31,* 499–516.

Vogt, W. P., & Johnson, R. B. (2011). *Dictionary of statistics and methodology: A nontechnical guide for the social sciences.* Los Angeles, CA: Sage.

Wenger, E. (1998). *Communities of practice: Learning, meaning, and identity.* Cambridge, England: Cambridge University Press.

Yorks, L. (2005). Nothing so practical as a good theory. *Human Resource Development Review, 4,* 111–113.

R. BURKE JOHNSON is a professor in the Department of Professional Studies at the University of South Alabama.

TRES STEFURAK is director of training for the Combined-Clinical & Counseling Psychology Ph.D. Program at the University of South Alabama.

Hesse-Biber, S. (2013). Thinking outside the randomized controlled trials experimental box: Strategies for enhancing credibility and social justice. In D. M. Mertens & S. Hesse-Biber (Eds.), *Mixed methods and credibility of evidence in evaluation. New Directions for Evaluation, 138,* 49–60.

5

Thinking Outside the Randomized Controlled Trials Experimental Box: Strategies for Enhancing Credibility and Social Justice

Sharlene Hesse-Biber

Abstract

Some evaluators employ randomized controlled trials (RCTs) as the gold standard of evidence-based practice (EBP). Critics of RCT designs argue that RCTs do not include the complexity of program participants' experiences or clinical expertise, and couple this with criticisms that it is difficult to transfer RCT findings from the laboratory to the real world of clinical practice. The evaluation questions applied to RCT designs often exclude issues related to participants' gender, race, class, and other differences, furthering the stereotyping process (Rogers & Ballantyne, 2009). I argue that weaving in a subjectivist methodology and shifting methodological perspectives and methods into RCT-based evaluations prior to, during, or after the RCT design serves to enhance the credibility and social-justice RCT praxis. ©Wiley Periodicals, Inc., and the American Evaluation Association.

W hen the concept of evidence-based practice (EBP) emerged in the field of medicine, it included three elements: clinical expertise, patient values in the decision-making practice, and best evidence from systematic research (Sackett, 2002; Sackett, Rosenberg, Gray,

Figure 5.1. Components of Evidence-Based Practice

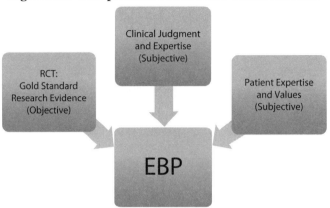

Source: Sackett et al.,1996; Sackett et al., 2000.

Haynes, & Richardson, 1996; Sackett, Straus, Richardson, Rosenberg, & Haynes, 2000). (See Figure 5.1.) The randomized controlled trial (RCT) was held up as the gold standard of methods design because it was thought to be the "best research" that employs a "sound methodology" (Sackett, 2002, p. 1).

However, over the past several decades, two important elements depicted in Figure 5.1 are increasingly dropping out of the EBP praxis model—*clinical judgment and expertise*, and *patient expertise and values*—leaving the praxis of EBP hyperfocused on a quantitative/experimental approach that is referred to as the gold standard.

EBP privileges a positivistic epistemology of knowledge building with an ontology that assumes social reality is out there and that truth can be ascertained through the careful praxis of the scientific method utilizing scientific objectivity. EBP takes up a narrow range of evaluation questions centering on testing particular RCT interventions that ascertain the effectiveness of an intervention. Outcome measures are conceptualized with the use of a binary understanding of the social reality—an intervention either worked or it didn't. Underlying RCT praxis, then, is a set of positivistic principles embedded into RCT.

Mixed Methods and RCT

The inclusion of qualitative methods was commonly practiced early on among evaluators (Cook & Reichardt, 1979; Shadish, Cook, & Leviton, 1991). However, the qualitative method often took a secondary role, centering a primarily quantitative evaluation. In addition, the qualitative method was delinked from its epistemological underpinnings (see Denzin & Lincoln, 2005; Guba, 1990; Howe, 2004).

Sandelowski (1996; see also Greene, Caracelli, & Graham, 1989) argues that the inclusion of a qualitative component can enhance the application of RCT laboratory findings by extending their application to naturalistic settings, specifically noting how the addition of a qualitative component into RCT could facilitate understanding how RCT findings transfer to a range of clinical settings.

There are few studies, however, that analyze just how evaluators utilize mixed method designs. A content analysis of mixed methods articles by Bryman (2006) notes the qualitative and quantitative components of a mixed methods project remain separate. Bryman (2007) conducted interviews with mixed methods researchers and found that they expressed a sense of confusion regarding how to integrate qualitative and quantitative methods, and that they lacked the skills to do this. Lewin, Glenton, and Oxman (2009) analyzed how qualitative methods are deployed alongside RCTs by conducting a content analysis of a systematic sample of 100 RCTs from the Cochrane EPOC (effective practice and organization of care) database for the years 2001–2003. They found only 30 of these trials had any linkage to a qualitative study, and even fewer used a theoretical perspective and/or provided any explanation for the integration of methods findings. The authors conclude that overall, the occurrence of qualitative methods is relatively uncommon in RCT research designs.

This article argues for thinking outside of the RCT experimental box by bringing back two of the original EBP components—patient and clinical expertise, and weaving multimethodologies and methods into current RCT praxis.

Re-Visioning RCT: Weaving and Shifting a Qualitative Component Into RCT Evaluation Designs

Weaving is a process of combining elements to form a complex entity whereby each makes its own equitable and important contribution toward enhancing the credibility of RCT findings. Shifting perspectives means the evaluator goes back and forth between different methodologies, linking them to the appropriate mix of methods. Thus, the evaluator traverses the subjective/objective knowledge-building continuum with the RCT component assuming a positivistic view of the social reality whose goal is the pursuit of the truth through the practice of the scientific method that utilizes practices to ensure a value-free, objective inquiry and a valid outcome. And within the same RCT space, the evaluator shifts closer to the other end of this continuum, by taking on a range of subjective methodological perspectives linked to a set of methods whose ontology favors a view of reality as multiple and whose goal is to understand multiple subjectivities.

We move now to a re-visioning of RCT design that weaves and shifts methodological and methods across the RCT process prior to, during, and after the RCT.

Prior to RCT

Prior to the RCT stage, the inclusion of a subjectivist methodology can weave a new set of questions that address *issues of representation*. There is currently a lack of critical recruitment strategies and little knowledge about what effective recruitment strategies can be utilized across different types of populations, especially when working with vulnerable populations (Froelicher & Lorig, 2002; Treweek et al., 2010). There is a need to identify those factors that can effectively engage participation at the recruitment phase. A subjectivist methodology asks questions that call for the inclusion of the voices of RCT participants and clinical experts whose experiences can contribute toward a broader understanding of issues of representation into conversation with traditional RCT designs. The inclusion of a subjective methodology focuses on the lived experiences of RCT participants and is mindful of the importance of also taking into account ethical issues involved in implementing the RCT design, as the following questions illustrate:

Does the target population interface well with the problem addressed in the program?
How well do recruitment procedures work?
To what extent does the target population reflect the range of diversity with regard to the overall goals of the project? Who is left out? Why?
To what extent is ethics praxis built into the recruitment and evaluation process?
How well does the target population understand what they are consenting to?
To what extent do participants accept the outcome(s) of randomization? Are participants willing to be randomized?

Questions emanating from weaving a subjectivist methodology prior to the RCT would also interrogate the nature, purpose, and implementation strategy of the RCT intervention and the lived experiences of both the target and clinical expertise linked to the RCT:

From whose perspective is the efficacy of an intervention determined?
To what extent is clinical expertise consulted when determining the intervention?
To what extent is the target population involved in assessing the efficacy and adherence potential of the intervention? Why or why not?
To what extent do the target population and clinical experts perceive the intervention as effective?
To what extent are the target populations' and clinical experts' voices incorporated into the RCT process overall?

These types of qualitatively driven questions prior to the RCT intervention are linked to qualitative methods in order to ascertain participants' lived experience with regard to issues of representation and intervention building to serve as a way to build inductively driven strategies for weaving marginalized voices seldom heard in the implementation of an RCT design. These overall sets of questions can also strengthen the ethical, social–psychological, and social-justice dimensions of the RCT itself, especially with regard to those questions that get at issues of representation, as well as the creation and selection of the specific intervention (see Forbes et al., 2011).

Some evaluators are beginning to weave multimethodologies and mix methods prior to the deployment of an RCT project. The Paramasivan, Huddart, and Hall (2011) evaluation of a recruitment program that serves men with prostate cancer reveals the importance of implementing a qualitative component prior to their RCT as a strategy for increasing recruitment. They collect and analyze qualitative data from an analysis of RCT protocol documents to assess recruitment effectiveness, conduct interviews with trial personnel and recruiters, and analyze audio recordings from recruitment appointments. The findings serve to train recruitment personnel prior to the recruitment phase of the RCT, with the goal of increasing the recruitment of males into the RCT.

Some evaluations of marginalized populations (see Feldstein, Ewing, Wray, Mead, & Adams, 2012) find a multimethodological perspective to be an effective strategy for engaging with the voices of participants in order to unearth their attitudes with regard to the efficacy of a specific intervention. The use of a particular subjectivist perspective that is action oriented can provide evaluators with a strategy for extending their inquiry to families and the wider community embedded in the target population. Corbie-Smith et al. (2010) used this strategy in their evaluation of an HIV prevention in two rural African American communities in the United States. Their RCT evaluation wove a subjective action-oriented methodology tied to a set of qualitative methods prior to the RCT, with the goal of producing multigenerational HIV prevention intervention strategies that incorporated the views and lived experiences from a broad range of members living in these communities. In addition, the evaluators also incorporated the expertise of clinicians and healthcare workers alongside participant and community voices in a process they term *intervention mapping* or IM. The use of more inclusive feedback from a subjectivist methodology such as participant action research, then, is one of several subjectivist perspectives that hold the promise of providing a range of feedback from different actors implicated in an RCT to assess the psychosocial and cultural context, while at the same time, retaining the validity of the RCT.

During the RCT

Weaving a subjective methodology linked to a qualitative method during RCT can capture understanding of the inner workings of the evaluation protocol and how it is administered, assess its ongoing impact on the target population, and keep track of who has dropped out of the RCT itself and why.

How well is the protocol followed by the RCT participants?
How well is the protocol administered, especially with regard to the intervention(s)?
Is there any slippage? Where and with what impact?
Is the protocol followed in an ethical manner?

Exploring these subjectively driven questions may require the evaluator to switch his or her use of methods from quantitative to qualitative to underscore that methods practices—their meaning and purpose in an evaluation process is linked to the questions they serve to address. In this case, a qualitative observational method can serve to provide the evaluator with experiential data that can be collected unobtrusively. Ethically administered observational methods may allow the evaluator to study the overall interactions taking place within the experimental context by embedding this qualitative component into the ongoing RCT without compromising the experimental design.

In addition, the findings from the qualitative component can provide important feedback to the ongoing evaluation such that an evaluator may take the findings from the embedded qualitative component to suggest on-the-fly strategies that might be applied to the ongoing RCT experimental protocol in order to make important midcourse adjustments to the design. After the trial, the findings from the embedded component can provide feedback to the RCT team, post-RCT, by suggesting strategies for enhancing future protocols. In addition, it would be important to assess overall issues of attrition of the target sample over the course of administering the RCT by asking questions such as: Who is leaving the trial? And why? These and earlier questions also center issues of social justice by focusing on the representation and well-being of the target population during the RCT. The findings from exploring these questions can then be woven into the RCT design process with the goal of enhancing future validity, trustworthiness, and ethics of the RCT results, and can also be fed back into any continuing or similar RCT evaluations.

Post-RCT

Weaving in a subjectivist methodology that privileges the lived experiences of those most impacted by the intervention—the study participants and those expert clinicians and health care providers who are most directly involved in their treatment—can be done post-RCT. Doing so can serve to increase the efficacy of the intervention in future RCTs. Some indication of how this might be done comes from an evaluation conducted by Bird,

Arthur, and Cox (2009). They utilize a subjectivist methodology, the goal of which is to understand the lived experiences of the target population, as well as clinical staff who administered the RCT. The evaluators linked a semistructured interview with 15 trial participants and five clinicians at the conclusion of a trial that sought to evaluate a rehabilitation program whose goal was to enhance patient recovery post–stem-cell transplantation. The results of the analysis of these interviews disclosed important issues with the administering of the complex trial interventions, with both patients and staff expressing dissatisfaction with trial procedures, especially those with regard to randomization.

The following types of questions serve to assess the intervention by those most impacted—the target population and those clinicians administering the intervention:

In your opinion did the intervention work? If so, in what sense?
In your opinion, what didn't work, if anything?
Could the intervention have been improved in any way? If so, what suggestions do you have?

An evaluator might decide to link the answering of these questions to a qualitative method with the goal of conducting in-depth exit interviews with participants and clinicians. In addition, the evaluator might conduct follow-up interviews and/or focus groups with a sample from the target population, and/or a sample of clinicians who administered the intervention in the field post-RCT. The evaluator can then place the results of both sets of interviews into conversation with one another with the goal of strengthening overall RCT efficacy and adherence to intervention.

This initiative might be followed up with a joint focus group consisting of clinicians and those who are currently the target of the intervention. The evaluation of these findings would then be used to provide a feedback loop into the beginning of the next clinical trial phase for consideration in building the next RCT protocol and selection of the target and intervention to be tested.

The following case study allows us to get at the *process* of weaving and shifting methodologies and mixing methods into an RCT design in a more dynamic manner.

Putting Things Together: Evaluation Case Study

Puschel and Thompson (2011) evaluated mammography-screening compliance rates among women aged 50 and above in Santiago, Chile. In spite of introducing free mammography screening, the compliance rate for this age group was only 12% after 3 years of free screening. This study sought to redress the lack of response to free screenings and to understand the persistent low rate of compliance.

The evaluation design utilized is a multimethodological sequential mixed methods RCT evaluation that *wove a different methodology and set of questions linked to qualitative methods.* The first component of the design was a qualitatively driven approach derived from an interpretative methodology, the goal of which was to develop an intervention that incorporated the lived experiences of their target population—women 50–70 who are eligible for a mammographic screening. The authors wanted to understand their lived experiences and what they perceived to be some impediments to getting a mammography. The findings from this qualitatively driven component was then woven into the RCT design component. The goal of the qualitative component (methodology linked to method) was to ascertain grounded knowledge with which to construct an intervention strategy based on the target population's subjective reality. The evaluators used several qualitative methods. They deployed focus groups consisting of seven heterogeneous and homogeneous focus groups with 48 women who differed with regard to their screening experience (women had not had a mammogram; those who had a mammogram during the past 2 years; those diagnosed with breast cancer) with the use of a semistructured interview schedule as well as observational techniques and field notes. They employed a grounded theory analytical approach to structure their coding and analysis of these data with the intent of finding both barriers and facilitators to the breast-cancer screening process. Their qualitatively driven findings allowed them to develop a set of intervention strategies based on women's lived experiences with mammography screening that they then integrated into three intervention strategies in the RCT design.

The second component of the evaluation, the RCT itself, required the evaluators to shift their methodology and methods praxis to a quantitatively driven positivistic methodological approach linked to an experimental method to answer the question: Did the interventions work? The RCT-component question was designed to ascertain the efficacy of different intervention types whose outcome measure was whether or not the specific intervention led to an increase in mammography screening over a 6-month period.

They gathered a random sample of 500 women aged 50–70 who were registered at a community clinic in Santiago, Chile, who had not had a mammogram within the past 2 years. These women were then randomly assigned to one of three experimental (intervention) groups based on input from the qualitative component: (a) the "standard group," which consisted of women who were only given brief advice on mammography screening by their primary-care physician; (b) the low-intensity group consisting of women who received brief advice and mail contact; (c) the high-intensity group that received brief advice, mail contact, as well as personal outreach. Participants' screening was tracked by the electronic registry of mammograms performed during the period of the study. The authors found 6 months into the trial that the control group's screening percentage was 7%, compared to 52% in the low-intensity group and 70% in the high-intensity group.

The Chilean mammography-screening research project underscores the importance of taking a multimethodological (in this example weaving and shifting a subjective and positivist methodology) as well as a mixed methods RCT approach, especially when implementing national health care policies at the primary-care level. Utilizing a qualitatively driven component linked to a qualitative method prior to the RCT's quantitative component provides the evaluators with critical information regarding the type of implementation strategies that might be most effective with regard to their specific target population, especially taking into account the particular cultural context at the local primary-care level. The grounded intervention resulted in significant increases in the number of mammography screenings.

The case study underscores how important it is for evaluators to think outside the gold standard RCT experimental box. Linking specific methodologies with targeted methods and placing the results of one in conversation with another can provide evaluators with new knowledge about what interventions might work with specific targeted populations. It is important also to note that these two methodologies, alongside their specific methods praxis, appear to be given *the same level of importance* in that the qualitative component is not just viewed as an add-on.

Evaluators in this study were able to weave and shift their methodological lens to provide a set of new questions that resulted in a richer, more complete, and more credible understanding of a particular clinical intervention overall. This evaluation design also has an important social-justice component. This evaluation study design wove findings from each component, allowing evaluators to take national policy initiatives and apply them to the local level. The shifting and weaving of evaluation methodologies and methods allows evaluators to shed light on localized realities that remained subjugated under a national health care social policy agenda, and in this case study, led to effective localized interventions.

In addition, this case study may be an important template of sorts (being mindful always of different localized conditions, specific geographical location—rural vs. urban settings, for example) that starts a national and local health care dialogue about how to connect national to local health care initiatives, being mindful of cultural diversity.

Conclusions

The practice model of evidence-based evaluation, especially those studies that employ a traditional RCT design, often assume a methods-centric approach that privileges the method of RCT as the component that will provide the most credible findings, and there is the implicit assumption of a single positivistic methodology. However, as I have demonstrated in this in-depth case study, it is critical to ask a range of different questions that stem from different methodological perspectives as critical components in determining the overall credibility of an evaluation RCT. It also requires a valuing of what different methodologies and methods can bring to an RCT design and gives equitable status to each contribution. Asking first what it is that we want to know (the question or set of questions), rather than rushing to the gold-standard praxis of RCT, can prevent having the method drive the evaluation study. It provides for the asking of new questions that address issues of difference and overall issues of social justice in RCT praxis: Who is included and excluded from the RCT recruitment phase and why? Whose agenda is served by asking this particular question? Who decided on this particular intervention?

The in-depth case study provided demonstrates how important it is for evaluators to tend to the context of discovery—that component of the evaluation process whereby the questions of the evaluation are framed—and it is this part of any evaluation project that also contributes to the overall credibility of RCT evidence. This case study also shows how important it is to place the contexts of discovery (where questions are framed) and the context of justification (method/analysis/interpretation employed to answer evaluation question) in conversation with one other by using the information from the context of discovery to inform the context of justification.

This case study does not search for a single truth, but instead seeks to capture a more complex understanding of the evaluation problem. The evaluators accomplish this by switching their methodological perspective (which often involves tempering their singular conception of truth through the process of negotiating truth in order to seek the variable conditions under which their findings apply or are transferable to different social contexts). In effect, they employ diverse methodological standpoints at different times within their RCT mixed methods design—never mixing up methodologies, but with an awareness of how specific methodologies are linked to their specific questions and methods choices.

This article provides strategies for strengthening the credibility of RCT with the use of a mixed methods approach that weaves and shifts multiple paradigms that ask new questions before, during, and after an RCT. These questions derive from new theoretical lenses (subjectivist in orientation) designed to upend the methods-centric praxis of RCT evaluations, by challenging RCT's traditional praxis with the goal of linking RCT more tightly to theory and the context of evaluation findings. Such a new praxis, as we have observed in the several studies addressed in this article, allows the RCT process to become more transparent, reflexive, and accountable. All of these strategies enrich the RCT evaluation process and lead to a complexity of understandings, which in turn serves to move the RCT praxis toward more credible evidence.

Advancing adoption of multimethodology/mixed methods strategies requires mixed methods training and familiarity with multimethodologies.

This will necessitate that evaluators employ an interdisciplinary team-based approach that requires team members to weave and shift their methods and methodologies. Team members should reach beyond their disciplinary comfort zones and use re-visioning and dialoguing across differing points of view in the service of enhancing credibility and social justice, thereby forging a new vision of what can lie outside the experimental RCT box.

References

Bird, L. A., Arthur, S., & Cox, K. (2009). "Did the trial kill the intervention?" Experiences from the development, implementation and evaluation of a complex intervention. *International Journal of Behavioral Medicine, 16*(3), 287–293. doi:10.1007/s12529-008-9017-1

Bryman, A. (2006). Integrating quantitative and qualitative research: How is it done? *Qualitative Research, 6,* 97–113.

Bryman, A. (2007). Barriers to integrating quantitative and qualitative research. *Journal of Mixed Methods Research, 1*(8), 8–22.

Cook, T. D., & Reichardt, C. S. (Eds.). (1979). *Qualitative and quantitative methods in evaluation research.* Thousand Oaks, CA: Sage.

Corbie-Smith, G., Akers, A., Blumenthal, C., Council, B., Wynn, M., Muhammad, M., & Stith, D. (2010). Intervention mapping as a participatory approach to developing an HIV prevention intervention in rural African American communities. *AIDS Education and Prevention, 2*(3), 184–202.

Denzin, N. K., & Lincoln, Y. S. (Eds.). (2005). *The Sage handbook of qualitative research* (3rd ed.). Thousand Oaks, CA: Sage.

Feldstein, S. W., Ewing, S., Wray, A. M., Mead, H. K., & Adams, S. K. (2012). Two approaches to tailoring treatment for cultural minority adolescents. *Journal of Substance Abuse Treatment, 43*(2), 190–203.

Forbes, L., Nicholls, C., Linsell, L., Graham, J., Tompkins, C., & Ramirez, A. J. (2011). Involving users in the design of a randomised controlled trial of an intervention to promote early presentation in breast cancer: Qualitative study. *BMC Medical Research Methodology, 11*(1), 24. doi:10.1186/1471-2288-11-24

Froelicher, E. S., & Lorig, K. (2002). Who cares about recruitment anyway? *Patient Education and Counseling, 48,* 97. doi:10.1016/S0738-3991(02)00168-4

Greene, J. C., Caracelli, V. J., & Graham, W. F. (1989). Toward a conceptual framework for mixed-method evaluation designs. *Educational Evaluation and Policy Analysis, 11,* 255–274.

Guba, E. G. (1990). The alternative paradigm dialog. In E. G. Guba (Ed.), *The paradigm dialog.* Newbury Park, CA: Sage.

Howe, K. R. (2004). A critique of experimentalism. *Qualitative Inquiry, 10*(1), 42–61.

Lewin, S., Glenton, C., & Oxman, A. D. (2009). Use of qualitative methods alongside randomised controlled trials of complex healthcare interventions: Methodological study. *British Medical Journal, 339,* b3496.

Paramasivan, S., Huddart, R., & Hall, E. (2011). Key issues in recruitment to randomised controlled trials with very different interventions: A qualitative investigation of recruitment to the SPARE trial. *Trials, 12,* 78.

Puschel, K., & Thompson, B. (2011). Mammogram screening in Chile: Using mixed methods to implement policy planning at the primary care level. *The Breast, 20,* 540–545.

Rogers, W., & Ballantyne, A. (2009). Justice in health research: What is the role of evidence-based medicine? *Perspectives in Biology and Medicine, 52*(2), 188–202.

Sackett, D. (2002). *Evidence-based medicine: How to practise and teach EBM* (2nd ed.). London, England: Churchill Livingstone.

Sackett, D. L., Rosenberg, W. M. C., Gray, J. A. M., Haynes, R. B., & Richardson, W. S. (1996). Evidence-based medicine: What it is and what it is not. *British Medical Journal, 312,* 71–72.

Sackett, D. L., Straus, S. E., Richardson, W. S., Rosenberg, W., & Haynes, R. B. (2000). *Evidence-based medicine: How to practice and teach EBM.* Edinburgh, Scotland: Churchill Livingstone.

Sandelowski, M. (1996). Using qualitative methods in intervention studies. *Research in Nursing & Health, 19,* 359–364.

Shadish, W. R., Cook, T. D., & Leviton, L. C. (1991). *Foundations of program evaluation: Theories of practice.* Newbury Park, CA: Sage.

Treweek, S., Pitkethly, M., Cook, J., Kjeldstrom, M., Taskila, T., Johansen, . . . Mitchell, E. (2010). Strategies to improve recruitment to randomised controlled trials. *Cochrane Database System Review 2010,* p. MR000013.

SHARLENE HESSE-BIBER is a professor of sociology at Boston College.

White, H. (2013). The use of mixed methods in randomized control trials. In D. M.
Mertens & S. Hesse-Biber (Eds.), *Mixed methods and credibility of evidence in evaluation.*
New Directions for Evaluation, 138, 61–73.

6

The Use of Mixed Methods in Randomized Control Trials

Howard White

Abstract

*Evaluations should be issues driven, not methods driven. The starting point
should be priority programs to be evaluated or policies to be tested. From this
starting point, a list of evaluation questions is identified. For each evaluation
question, the task is to identify the best available method for answering that question. Hence it is likely that any one study will contain a mix of methods.
A crucial question for an impact evaluation is that of attribution: What difference did the intervention make to the state of the world? (framed in any specific evaluation as the difference a clearly specified intervention or set of
interventions made to indicators of interest). For interventions with a large
number of units of assignment, this question is best answered with a quantitative experimental or quasi-experimental design. And for prospective, or ex
ante, evaluation designs a randomized control trial (RCT) is very likely to be
the best available method for addressing this attribution question if it is feasi-
ble. But just the attribution question will be answered. A high-quality impact
evaluation will answer a broader range of evaluation questions of a more process nature, both to inform design and implementation of the program being*

I thank Michael Bamberger, Thomas de Hoop, Nidhi Khattri, Lina Payne, and Daniel Phillips for helpful comments on an earlier version of the article, and Avanica Khosla for
assistance in the preparation of the article. The usual disclaimer applies.

evaluated and for external validity. Mixed methods combine the counterfactual analysis from an RCT with factual analysis with the use of quantitative and qualitative data to analyze the causal chain, drawing on approaches from a range of disciplines. The factual analysis will address such issues as the quality of implementation, targeting, barriers to participation, or adoption by intended beneficiaries. ©Wiley Periodicals, Inc., and the American Evaluation Association.

The use of randomized control trials (RCTs) to evaluate economic and social development programs has grown rapidly over the last decade. This rapid growth in evidence has begun to address the evaluation gap pointed out in the 2006 report *When Will We Ever Learn?* (Centre for Global Development, 2006), which argued that there is a lack of rigorous evidence as to which development programs are effective. In response to the CGD report, the International Initiative for Impact Evaluation (3ie) was created in 2008 to promote the production and use of high-quality impact evaluations of socioeconomic development interventions in low- and middle-income countries (see www.3ieimpact.org). Illustrating the growth in evidence, as of mid-2012, 3ie's impact-evaluation database contains over 800 studies with experimental and quasi-experimental designs.

But this trend has not been universally welcomed. Critics of the use of RCTs point to the fact that they only address one, limited, evaluation question, and that a broader range of evaluation approaches are available and should be used to address questions of relevance. But this view presents the issue as either/or, which is not the case. Rather RCTs should be embedded in a broader evaluation design, which combines the counterfactual analysis of attribution with a factual analysis across the causal chain.

The use of mixed methods in impact evaluation has previously been explored in a number of papers: H. White (2008) provides examples of mixed methods studies that used experimental and quasi-experimental designs, and he also developed a framework for mixed methods applied to impact evaluations of infrastructure projects (2011a). Bamberger et al. (2009) argue that the requirement for evaluations to address a broad range of questions is a feature of international development, and this fact opens the door to the use of mixed methods.

This article brings two contributions to this literature. The next section provides a defense of the black box, which rests on the different types of analysis RCTs bring to a mixed method impact evaluation compared to the perspectives provided by the factual analysis. The two approaches are complements, not alternatives. Then I elaborate on the argument that the mixing of methods is not mixing qualitative and quantitative approaches, but combining counterfactual and factual analysis, where the latter will usually draw on quantitative and qualitative data. To illustrate this point, I provide examples of mixed methods at various stages of the evaluation cycle, along with some reflections on the type of data used.

NEW DIRECTIONS FOR EVALUATION • DOI: 10.1002/ev

Conceptual Issues

The Black Box: Curse or Blessing?

RCTs establish a causal relationship between the intervention and the measured outcomes by statistical means. First, an eligible population is defined. A sample is taken from which units are assigned to treatment and control groups at random. Given a sufficiently large number of units of assignment, then we expect that the average characteristics of the treatment and control groups, both observed and unobserved, are the same. Baseline characteristics, the determinants of the outcomes of interest, and underlying trends in those determinants, will be the same in treatment and control, unless there is some fault in the design or the sample drawn is in the small percentage of cases for which there are significant differences between treatment and control. Hence, any observed differences between treatment and control in outcomes after the intervention must be attributed to the intervention. The simplest RCT compares a single treatment to an untreated control, but there are variations on this design, such as comparing different treatments of combinations thereof.

Of course there are possible threats to internal validity in randomized control trials, especially in a development setting in which the evaluators have limited control over the conditions for the experiment. Such threats include Hawthorne and John Henry effects, and spillovers and contamination (see H. White, 2011b), all of which need be recognized and dealt with. But the point being made here is to distinguish between the way in which a causal relationship is established with experimental (and quasi-experimental) methods, and the basis for doing so in other evaluation approaches.

Mechanism-based approaches are based on an assessment of the validity of the causal chain and the fidelity of implementation to establish a plausible association between the intervention and the outcomes (see H. White & Phillips, 2012 for further discussion). But for RCTs the causal chain is irrelevant, though I will provide caveats to this statement below. The causal chain is a black box, which we do not need to look inside to establish the causal link between intervention outcome (Figure 6.1).

The black-box approach is seen as a shortcoming of RCTs, an inability to explain why things work rather than merely if they do or not. But the black box is a blessing, not a curse.

Take the analogy of tossing a coin. For any one coin toss the trajectory is a function of the pressure applied, the starting position, air currents, and the point at which the coin is caught. Complex formulas could be applied to calculate whether a particular toss will come up heads or tails. But we need not understand any of that to know that, with sufficient tosses, the coin will come up heads close to half the time. More specifically there will be between 43 and 57 heads out of a hundred tosses just over 95 percent of the time. This is the power of statistics. We can make statements about

Figure 6.1. An RCT Theory of Change

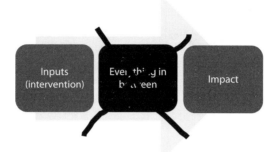

the outcomes of a complex phenomenon without any understanding of that phenomenon.

Similarly, an intervention may have complex causal pathways that defy easy analysis. Unlike other evaluation approaches, this complexity is not a problem for an RCT. The association between intervention and outcomes does not require any understanding of the causal chain.

So an RCT can establish the impact of an intervention even if we have no understanding of the causal chain, that is, it is too complex to unpick. When we do understand the causal chain we will still want a quantitative experimental (RCT) or quasi-experimental design to measure the magnitude of that impact, which is a necessary basis for cost-effectiveness analysis.

This is not to say that causal-chain analysis is irrelevant. Quite the opposite is the case. Mixed method causal-chain analysis should be undertaken as part of the overall evaluation, with an RCT used to address the attribution question and other approaches to answer evaluation questions from other parts of the causal chain. Without such an analysis the study will not be able to address crucial questions on policy relevance such as whether the failure to have an impact results from design failure or implementation failure. Furthermore, the contextual analysis implied in the theory-based impact evaluation approach strengthens external validity, which may be weaker or absent in a bare-bones RCT.

What Are Mixed Methods?

Evaluation discourse distinguishes approaches, methods, and tools (H. White & Phillips, 2012). The mixed methods approach combines different methods, each of which has its own tools.

Mixed methods are often seen as quantitative and qualitative. But in impact evaluation the important distinction is between factual and counterfactual analysis. Factual analysis captures what happened. Counterfactual analysis captures what would have happened in the absence of the intervention. As shown in Table 6.1, counterfactual analysis may be carried out

Table 6.1. Mixed Methods: Types and Uses

	Quantitative	*Qualitative*
Factual	Causal-chain analysis, for example, compliance rates, targeting, and tests of knowledge	Causal-chain analysis, for example, participatory processes, reasons for noncompliance
Counterfactual	Large n attribution analysis Small n attribution analysis	Small n attribution analysis

Figure 6.2. Different Analysis at Different Levels of the Causal Chain

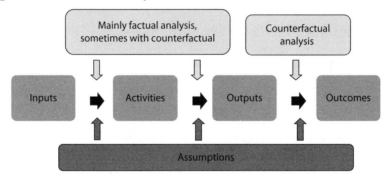

using either quantitative or qualitative data, the appropriate method depending on the evaluation questions being addressed.

Mixed methods is sometimes presented as an approach that combines perspectives from different disciplines, e.g., anthropology and economics. I do not see that as an alternative definition, but a practice that is implied in the appropriate combination of factual and counterfactual data and analysis.

The counterfactual analysis is most usually concerned with the final link in the causal chain, that is, attribution analysis with respect to outcomes (see Figure 6.2). Where there are a large number of units of assignment, then statistical large n methods are the most appropriate methods. These are quantitative methods, that is, experimental or quasi-experimental designs. Where the number of units of assignment is small, then small n analysis should be used, which may draw on both quantitative and qualitative data (H. White & Phillips, 2012).

Factual data are used for causal-chain analysis from inputs to outputs, though sometimes counterfactual analysis may be used for output variables, or even lower down the causal chain. As listed in Table 6.1, these factual data are either quantitative or qualitative, depending on the question. Some factual data may come from the monitoring system, though

NEW DIRECTIONS FOR EVALUATION • DOI: 10.1002/ev

such data are only available from treatment areas and may be subject to biases. Survey data should collect quantitative process data regarding the evaluation. Although process questions do not apply to the comparison areas, data from these sites need to cover more than just outcomes and matching variables. In particular, information is needed of other ongoing interventions to capture possible contamination.

As emphasized in Figure 6.2, theory-based causal-chain analysis is not simply a case of tracking indicators at the different levels or stages of a logic model. It is a rigorous empirical assessment of causal mechanisms and the assumptions underlying the causal chain. The need for rigor applies to both factual and counterfactual data, and to qualitative and quantitative data (see H. White, 2002, for an elaboration of this point). Rigor applies both to data collection and analysis.

The Use of Different Methods in a Single Study

There is an essential difference in the philosophical approach of the counterfactual analysis of attribution and the causal-chain analysis. The former is inductive reasoning and the latter deductive. That is, subject to satisfying the requirements of the method, identifying a causal relationship using an experimental or quasi-experimental approach constitutes proof that such a relationship exists, subject of course to the internal validity issues and the small chance of a bad sample mentioned above.

Causal-chain analysis, relying on assembling evidence in support of a set of relationships, cannot claim the same level of proof (see also H. White & Phillips, 2012). The arguments may seem convincing, but they can be wrong. The usual way to strengthen a deductive argument is to elaborate, and empirically discount, alternative plausible explanations, which is indeed the heart of Scriven's general elimination methodology (e.g., Scriven, 2008).

Although such techniques should also be applied in a theory-based impact evaluation, the mixing of methods in an impact evaluation has a more powerful approach. Mixed methods combine the inductive and deductive. The experimental design trumps the alternative explanations, demonstrating conclusively the link from inputs to outcomes, though of course it may not be the sole determinant of those outcomes (see H. White, 2010a, for an elaboration of the point that attribution need not mean sole attribution).

Examples of Mixed Method Causal-Chain Analysis

Setting Out the Evaluation Framework

It is now commonly accepted that the starting point for an evaluation is to set out the theory of change (Ravallion, 2009; Rogers, 2009). The theory of change leads to the identification of the evaluation questions (H. White, 2010b). One of these questions will be about impact, that is, what difference the intervention makes. Where there are a large number of units of assign-ment, answering the impact question is best done with the use of a counter-factual analysis based on an experimental or quasi-experimental design.

But there are many other evaluation questions that require a factual analysis. An evaluation of the intervention requires answering all evalua-tion questions by the most appropriate means. The shortcoming of many RCTs, that they address only the impact question whilst ignoring other evaluation questions of interest, is not inherent in RCTs. Rather, RCTs can and should be embedded in a broader evaluation framework that addresses questions across the causal chain. For example, qualitative data will often help interpret results from quantitative analysis. The purpose of this section is to give examples as to how this may be done.

As stated above, the starting point is sketching out the theory of change, how it is that the intervention will achieve the planned outcomes. The theory of change is situated within the socio-economic context that mediates the causal relationships. Qualitative data are used to provide this understanding of context (Garbarino & Holland, 2009).

Develop Hypothesis and Identify Instrumental Variables

Development of the theory of change is based entirely or largely on quali-tative data—project documents, evaluations of similar interventions, and speaking to project staff and sector specialists. Participatory methods may be used at the community level to identify desired or expected outcomes (Chambers, 2009). Diverse sources of data can inform identification of outcomes.

The day I was due to make a presentation on mixed methods in Delhi, the *Times of India* carried a story with the headline "Highway to hell: Village sees 20 deaths in 3 years." The story was a salutary reminder of what roads do: roads kill people. It is of course an unintended out-come, but it is one that should not be ignored in the evaluation of road construction and improvement projects. Indeed, the development of cost–benefit analysis in developed countries was precisely to incorporate the costs of such negative externalities into decision making for investment projects. However, I am only aware of one impact evaluation, by the Asian Development Bank, which takes accidents into account in assessing road improvements.

While studying rural electrification in Laos, I was taken to visit an off-grid solar-panel program. The curious thing on paper was that the off-grid program was in one part of a village, the rest of which was connected to the grid. The site visit readily explained this apparent puzzle, because the unconnected households lived on an island in the middle of the Mekong River. However, I learned that half the 30 households on the village had moved to the mainland since the arrival of the grid so as to enjoy grid elec-tricity. That is, location is endogenous. People move to enjoy better facilities. An impact-evaluation design that ignores this fact may well suffer selection bias.

Other times, identification may not be so obvious. A livelihoods project in India supported by the U.K. Department for International Development (DFID) allocated funds to be shared amongst self-help groups (SHGs) according to watersheds. Most villages were based in one watershed, though some had land in two catchment areas and so got more funds. In any case, the allocation of funds was unrelated to village size. Hence smaller villages had more funds to go around. Women joined SHGs to access funds. In larger villages, there was far less chance of obtaining these funds, so participation rates could be expected to be lower. Hence village size serves as an identifying variable.

Another insight regarding participation in the same project came from following Chambers's advice to watch out for angry people (Chambers, 2009). The "angry man in Andhra Pradesh" was angry because his daughter had been a member of an SHG for more than 2 years and never received a loan. The reason was clear. The daughter was unmarried and living with her parents. Her mother was a member of the same group and had received a loan. As far as the group was concerned, the loan is a loan to the household, not the individual. I took what the angry man told me back to the survey data, and found a clear negative relationship between the participation rate and the number of eligible women in the household; and more than two-thirds of women live in households with two or more eligible members.

Questionnaire Design and Improved Data Collection

Being in the field informs questionnaire design. Going back to the Laos example, before my visit I had been puzzling over a data set to model which communities had access to grid electricity. Surprisingly, an ethnic dummy variable was significant, but the overall explanatory power was low. The visit to the village described above explained this puzzle. As mentioned, the community did not have grid electricity, because it was on an island. Other communities were not connected to the grid because they were located in mountainous regions. Those ethnic groups concentrated in island and mountainous areas were less likely to be connected to the grid. Unfortunately, neither the household nor community questionnaire had collected these location data, which most likely would have been done had there been a visit to the field before finalizing the questionnaire.

A second example comes from the SHGs in India, for which we collected two rounds of data. At the second round, it was evident that participation in self-help groups had declined, from around 50 to 40 percent of eligible women. We identified reasons for this drop through qualitative work. Had we done qualitative work before the second round of data collection, we would have been able to capture the characteristics of women who had dropped out and their reasons for doing so. So scoping qualitative fieldwork is useful not just prior to baseline, but also between survey rounds.

Knowledge of field conditions can improve questionnaire design, for example, the importance of festivals and labor exchange as a source of protein in diets (see H. White, 2002). But mixed methods also mean thinking creatively about data collection. Behavioral games, based on psychology, are increasingly used to get more accurate measures of intangibles such as cooperative behavior, social cohesion, and risk adversity (Cardenas & Carpenter, 2008). Vignettes have also proved a more reliable means of measuring empowerment rather than a straightforward question with a Likert scale (King & Wand, 2007). Qualitative methods may also generate data that may be coded for quantitative analysis (Chambers, 2009).

Implementation Failure Versus Design Failure

It is important to understand if a program is being implemented correctly or not. If not, then expected outcomes will not be realized because of problems in implementation; maybe the program design is sound, though we cannot be sure. But the study can point to the implementation failure to be addressed by program staff.

A nutrition program in Bangladesh provided both nutritional counseling to mothers of young children and supplementary feeding (H. White, 2010b; H. White & Masset, 2006). But impact was undermined by both design and implementation failures. On the design front, the failure to provide information about the program to mothers-in-law and husbands undermined the impact of nutritional counseling, as these household members are key decision makers in obtaining and using food. The effectiveness of supplementary feeding was reduced by mistargeting, resulting in part from the inability of the village fieldworkers to read the growth charts intended to screen children for entry into the program.

Another case of implementation failure was uncovered during the monitoring of a preschool program in Latin America. It was found that many of the children of poor households were not attending preschool. Phone calls to parents and project staff revealed that preschool staff members were turning away children if they had missed some days due to sickness. This was not the idea at all, and this practice was stopped by communicating with preschools.

These examples illustrate a range of qualitative data. The original insight into decision making in joint households in rural Bangladesh came from reading anthropological studies (notably, S. White, 1992). This insight was taken back into the quantitative analysis through coding the household roster to create a variable identifying women living with their mothers-in-law. Follow-up focus groups confirmed the importance of this issue. Fieldworkers were tested with actual growth charts: a straightforward piece of factual analysis that uncovered a crucial weak link in the causal chain. The phone calls to project staff and parents were an ad hoc form of data collection, which successfully uncovered an implementation problem.

What all these examples demonstrate is the iteration that occurs in a good mixed methods approach. Impact-evaluation budgets should include funds for work whose scope will be determined as the study proceeds.

Fidelity of Evaluation Design

Evaluation designs are frequently compromised in the field. Contamination, in which similar programs and programs affecting similar outcomes get carried out in the comparison areas, is a common cause. Data are needed on the nature and extent of contamination so that it can be dealt with if possible.

In China, eyeglasses were distributed to secondary-school students who needed them, helping to improve their test scores. However, end-line data showed increased use of eyeglasses in six comparison townships (Glewwe, Park, & Zhao, 2012). Discussions with project staff showed that the doctors doing the eye tests had glasses left over from the treatment townships, so gave them away in the comparison communities. The study had used a matched-pair randomization design and so was able to drop the pairs with contaminated controls with no risk of bias. This example shows the importance of collecting appropriate data along the causal chain in both treatment and comparison areas.

In India, the evaluation of an HIV/AIDS program targeted at high-risk groups was undermined when the implementing agency decided to go ahead and roll out the program statewide halfway through the pilot (Samuels & McPherson, 2010). Hence there was no difference in HIV/AIDS prevalence in treatment and control, though it has come down in both. Whether this was because of the project was impossible to determine as both treatment and control had been treated.

Understand How Something Works (or Why It Does Not)

An analysis of textbooks in Kenya found that they had no impact on learning outcomes. Other data showed that many children could not read the textbooks, as they were too difficult, and children's English language skills were too poor to understand the books. Subgroup analysis showed that children with higher baseline test scores did indeed benefit from the textbooks (Glewwe, Kremer, & Moulin, 2009).

This example provides a case of iteration between methods. It also provides an example of the caveat I mentioned earlier regarding RCTs not being able to open the black box. One way in which they can do so is through subgroup analysis, identifying who benefits and who does not. As this example shows, such subgroup analysis sheds light on the causal chain. Overreliance on subgroup analysis can open the door to data mining.

Ideally the subgroups to be examined are specified by the theory of change before the data analysis begins, but allowance should be made for new subgroups identified by the iteration between theory and data.

Social funds mobilize the community to identify, manage, and help implement community projects. Analysis of the household data in Malawi and Zambia showed that households contribute to making bricks but not decisions. That is, participation rates were high in assisting with physical construction, but far fewer villagers knew a meeting had taken place to select the project, still fewer attended that meeting, and a small minority spoke at the meeting. Brief field visits to 17 communities, lasting around 2 hours per community, revealed a common pattern. Social funds were not creating social capital; rather, they were using the social capital of traditional social structures of village headmen to mobilize households to make bricks, with a system of local fines for enforcement (see Vajja & White, 2008, for more discussion). This was not elite capture, but an efficient way of harnessing the community to deliver small-scale infrastructure. So in this case, the qualitative data from field trips helped understand the pattern found in the household survey data.

In the social-fund case factual analysis is used to analyze meeting attendance; there is no sense at looking at meeting attendance in the comparison group. But if the design were comparing two different participatory approaches, the counterfactual analysis of process-level indicators would be appropriate. So, although counterfactual analysis is often focused on the outcome level, that is not necessarily the case. It is sometimes used at other levels of the causal chain. But it should only be used when it is sensible to do so—one World Bank study used a comparison group to show that rehabilitated schools had better facilities than nonrehabilitated schools. In that case a before-versus-after factual analysis of the improvement from rehabilitation would have been more appropriate.

A final example comes from developed countries. Scared Straight is a program aimed at juveniles that exposes youth at risk to a short spell of prison life, the theory being that they will be sufficiently put off by the experience to go straight. Unfortunately for this theory, a systematic review has shown that the program does not work. At best it has no impact, but in some cases youth exposed to the program are more likely to turn to a life of crime than those in the control group. Qualitative data reveals why: (a) some youth actually enjoyed the structure and facilities of prison life, (b) they saw the prisoners as role models, and (c) people they met inside gave them criminal contacts on the outside. Once again, qualitative data help to understand quantitative results.

Presenting Results: The Power of the Anecdote

Finally, anecdotes can be used to illustrate study findings. Policy makers are more convinced by human-interest presentations rather than statistical

NEW DIRECTIONS FOR EVALUATION • DOI: 10.1002/ev

analysis. And indeed, international development agencies, from the largest multilateral to the smallest NGO, promote their effectiveness through heartwarming success stories. The responsibility of the researcher is to ensure that such anecdotes are consistent with the evidence, rather than contrary to it.

Conclusions

It is wrong to posit that there is a choice between RCTs and other evaluation approaches. RCTs are the best available method to answer the attribution question when an ex ante design is possible and there are a large number of units of assignment, and provided there are no other obstacles to a randomized design. But the average treatment effect provided by an RCT only answers the attribution question. Other approaches are complements rather than alternatives. The counterfactual analysis of attribution with random assignment should be complemented by factual analysis utilizing both quantitative and qualitative data to address questions and interrogate assumptions across the causal chain.

This article has stressed that mixed methods combine counterfactual with factual analysis, where the latter includes both quantitative and qualitative data. But it has also argued that qualitative data comes from a wide range of sources. The usual reaction of researchers to adding a qualitative component is wrong on two counts. First, this component usually comprises a few focus groups. But the range of qualitative data is far wider, from project reports to anthropological studies, and from telephone calls and brief field visits to utilizing the full range of participatory methods, of which focus groups are just a small component. The second is that the researchers add a qualitative component but do not truly integrate it in any meaningful way.

Drawing on mixed methods will produce studies that answer evaluation questions across the causal chain, thus determining not only what works but why and how to make it work better. The use of mixed methods, theory-based impact-evaluation designs will, by informing better policies and programs, and save lives.

References

Bamberger, M., Rao, V., & Woolcock, M. (2009). *Using mixed methods in monitoring and evaluation: Experiences from international development* (Working Paper No. 107). Retrieved from http://www.bwpi.manchester.ac.uk/resources/Working -Papers/bwpi-wp-10709
Cardenas, J. C., & Carpenter, J. (2008). Behavioural development economics: Lessons from field labs in the developing world. *Journal of Development Studies*, 44(3), 311–338.
Centre for Global Development. (2006). *When will we ever learn? Improving lives through impact evaluation*. Washington, DC: Centre for Global Development. Retrieved from http://www.cgdev.org/files/7973_file_WillWeEverLearn.pdf

Chambers, R. (2009). So that the poor count more: Using participatory methods for impact evaluation. *Journal of Development Effectiveness, 1*(3), 243–246.

Garbarino, S., & Holland, J. (2009). *Quantitative and qualitative methods in impact evaluation and measuring results* (Issues Paper). Retrieved from http://www.gsdrc.org/docs/open/EIRS4.pdf

Glewwe, P., Kremer, M., & Moulin, S. (2009). Many children left behind? Textbooks and test scores in Kenya. *American Economic Journal: Applied Economics, 1*(1), 112–135.

Glewwe, P., Park, A., & Zhao, M. (2012). *Visualizing development: Eyeglasses and academic performance in rural primary schools in China* (Working Paper No. 12–2). Retrieved from http://ageconsearch.umn.edu/handle/120032

King, G., & Wand, J. (2007). Comparing incomparable survey responses: New tools for anchoring vignettes. *Political Analysis, 15*(1), 46–66.

Ravallion, M. (2009). Evaluating three stylised interventions. *Journal of Development Effectiveness, 1*(3), 227–236.

Rogers, P. (2009). Matching impact evaluation design to the nature of the intervention and the purpose of the evaluation. *Journal of Development Effectiveness, 1*(3), 217–226.

Samuels, F., & McPherson, S. (2010). Meeting the challenge of proving impact in Andhra Pradesh, India. *Journal of Development Effectiveness, 2*(4), 468–485.

Scriven, M. (2008). A summative evaluation of RCT methodology and an alternative approach to causal research. *Journal of Multidisciplinary Evaluation, 5*(9), 11–24.

Vajja, A., & White, H. (2008). Can the World Bank build social capital? The experience of social funds in Malawi and Zambia. *Journal of Development Studies, 44*(8), 1145–1168.

White, H. (2002). Combining quantitative and qualitative approaches in poverty analysis. *World Development, 30*(3), 511–522.

White, H. (2008). Of probits and participation: The use of mixed methods in quantitative impact evaluation. *IDS Bulletin, 39*(1), 98–189.

White, H. (2010a). A contribution to current debates in impact evaluation. *Evaluation, 16*(2), 153–164.

White, H. (2010b). Theory-based impact evaluation: principles and practice. *Journal of Development Effectiveness, 1*(3), 271–284.

White, H. (2011a). Achieving high-quality impact evaluation design through mixed methods: The case of infrastructure. *Journal of Development Effectiveness, 3*(1), 131–144.

White, H. (2011b). *An introduction to the use of randomized control trials to evaluate development interventions* (Working Paper No. 9). Retrieved from http://www.3ieimpact.org/en/evaluation/working-papers/working-paper-9/

White, H., & Masset, E. (2006). The Bangladesh Integrated Nutrition Program: Findings from an impact evaluation. *Journal of International Development, 19*, 627–652.

White, H., & Phillips, D. (2012). *Addressing attribution of cause and effect in small n impact evaluations: Towards an integrated framework* (Working Paper No. 15). Retrieved from http://www.3ieimpact.org/en/evaluation/working-papers/working-paper-15/

White, S. (1992). *Arguing with the crocodile: Gender and class in Bangladesh.* London, England: Zed Books.

HOWARD WHITE *is the executive director of the International Initiative for Impact Evaluation (3ie).*

Frost, N., & Nolas, S.-M. (2013). The contribution of pluralistic qualitative approaches to mixed methods evaluations. In D. M. Mertens & S. Hesse-Biber (Eds.), *Mixed methods and credibility of evidence in evaluation. New Directions for Evaluation, 138*, 75–84.

7

The Contribution of Pluralistic Qualitative Approaches to Mixed Methods Evaluations

Nollaig Frost, Sevasti-Melissa Nolas

Abstract

There is a strong trend in policy-making circles for strategic, systemic, and large-scale interventions. Although such trends make sense in terms of economy of scale and scope, the political will necessary for making these large-scale interventions a reality is often lacking, and the problem of the transferability of interventions from one local context to another (e.g., from trial conditions to local communities, and then across local communities) remains largely unsolved (Cartwright & Munro, 2010). ©Wiley Periodicals, Inc., and the American Evaluation Association.

On the ground what we find are many small-scale social-change efforts. Such change is not exempt from the need to be accountable to stakeholders such as service users, funders, and practitioners, who often express a wish to learn from their change efforts in order to improve them. Yet experimental or epidemiological approaches that are preferred for large-scale interventions are unsuitable for these smaller projects, especially new and innovative ones, as they fail to answer questions of process (how does it work?), salience (does it matter?), appropriateness (is this the right service for *these* children?), and satisfaction (are users, providers, and other stakeholders satisfied with the service?) (Hansen & Rieper, 2009).

These are exactly the sorts of questions from which small-scale interventions, especially new and innovative ones, benefit most, as they hold the promise of developing a richer, multiperspective, and multidimensional understanding of the particularities of the context in which social interventions are delivered. New interventions often develop from small ideas, therefore requiring a great deal of work in terms of proof of concept and program theory development in order to attract more funding and to be rolled out on a wider basis. Conversely, the contexts of intervention delivery vary widely across communities, even within proximal geographic areas. Furthermore, intervention spaces are often contested spaces. Social problems are variously defined depending on the perspective being adopted (e.g., policy, practitioners, user), and social interventions are often preceded by prolonged negotiation of how to define, act, and ascribe value to social problems (Guba & Lincoln, 1989; Mosse, 2005; Pressman & Wildavsky, 1973). As such, it is these intervention projects, and the spaces they create, that are the most suitable candidates for qualitatively driven mixed-methods evaluation approaches, by which we mean evaluation approaches that draw on the logic of qualitative inquiry and account for the dynamics of social process, change, and social context (Mason, 2006). Furthermore, as the welfare state contracts in many Western economies (the main consumers of evaluation) and localized agendas proliferate, small-scale change is likely to become the recognized norm and the need for (qualitatively driven) mixed methods evaluations will become even more important and widespread.

The arrival of the evidence-based movement on both sides of the Atlantic has heralded a new era in which qualitative inquiry for evaluation is once again overshadowed by large-scale quantitative measurement. To those untrained in qualitative methodologies and methods it is easy to confuse the interpretative practices that are at the heart of these methods with little more than personal opinion, which is of no use to credible and trustworthy evaluation. Such misunderstandings have led to long, bitter, and ultimately unproductive methods wars, which detract attention from phenomena of interest, namely, the needs of social-intervention efforts themselves, which are wide and varied. In the interim, advocates of qualitative methods, seizing on the challenge of having been relegated to the basement of the hierarchy of evidence, have made leaps and bounds over the last decade when it comes to demonstrating quality and rigor. The development of theory-driven research, of triangulation and reflexivity in qualitative research, and of the application of clear and systematic models of analysis (e.g., Emerson & Frosh, 2004; Frost, 2009) has enhanced the transparency of qualitative methods, meaning that qualitative research, applied in these ways, offers a wealth of possibilities to evaluators.

In this article we aim to extend the debate about the use of qualitative methods in mixed methods evaluation to show how they can enhance the efficiency and effectiveness of social interventions across the board. We call this approach *pluralistic qualitative evaluation* (PQE), and argue that using qualitative methods pluralistically in mixed methods evaluation can bring a more holistic insight to social interventions, and insights that more closely represent the complexity of human experience and meaning making. We illustrate how rich, multilayered insight to experience can be obtained with this approach, and how the process of reaching this outcome is by necessity transparent and accountable. We support the importance of this approach to evaluation with the use of a study that explores youth participation in a youth inclusion program (Nolas, 2008). We demonstrate ways in which the pluralistic approach enables evaluation of the program, and will link key considerations within a framework of transformative evaluation (Mertens, 2009), which highlights the value of responsive processes through consideration of relationships between methods, and between evaluators and stakeholders.

Using Qualitative Methods in Evaluation

Using a single qualitative method for evaluation is virtually unheard of within traditional hierarchy-of-evidence approaches, where qualitative research is positioned just above opinion. At first glance this is easy to understand. For evaluation to have an impact on decision makers, there is a need for data that are reliable and understandable (Robson, 2002). The varying interests of the stakeholder groups invested in the evaluation and its outcomes often means that different members prioritize different aspects of the evaluation. Evaluation of a typical top-down planned approach to social change will be of interest to an audience that includes representatives from groups of high-level decision makers such as policy makers, professionals implementing the program or policy, and service users accessing the program. Those developing and delivering the program may be more interested in the resources necessary to ensure its high quality. Those participating in the program may be more focused on how participation can enhance their well-being. This variation in perception and investment means that outcomes must be presented in ways that are relevant to the diversity of the audience, and the process by which they are reached must be comprehensive, accountable, and transparent. Researchers have pointed to the value of qualitative research in providing depth and perspective with the use of soft measures. Quality-assessment criteria relevant to methods that seek to access subjective meaning ensure its credibility. Chief amongst the quality-assessment criteria is that of reflexivity, in which the evaluators place themselves within the inquiry process. Paradigms that regard realities as constructed through social interaction are common in qualitative approaches, and awareness of the role of the evaluator is regarded as essential.

Acknowledging that seeking to generalize evaluation outcomes risks obscuring marginalized voices or local contexts enables innovative ways to evaluate the needs of those who commission, deliver, and receive social interventions. A typology-of-evidence approach (e.g., Petticrew & Roberts, 2003; Petticrew & Roberts, 2006) moves away from the constraints of the traditional hierarchy of evidence in which randomized control trials (RCTs) are held as the gold standard and experimental designs are widely employed to compare groups. Instead, it allows better exploration of the complexity of social interventions by promoting a focus on the relative contributions that different kinds of methods can make to different kinds of research questions. It seeks to identify the issues key to the evaluation, and to the various stakeholders in the evaluation, and to match them with the most appropriate research design. It allows questions not answerable with quantitative measures—such as "How does it work?" and "Does it matter?"—to be asked. Questions of outcome and cost effectiveness are left to other designs. With the careful consideration of appropriateness of design and question, a typology-of-evidence approach allows for the multiple and changeable needs of social interventions to be evaluated in a rigorous and systematic manner. Combining qualitative methods to address these questions acknowledges that the evaluation of effectiveness is comprised of different sorts of knowledge and requires different questions and designs to address them comprehensibly.

It is our argument that the adoption of a multiontological and multi-epistemological approach allows for multiple realities and worldviews to be the focus of social-intervention evaluation. In the rest of this article, we describe how the use of multiple qualitative methods in evaluation can be an appropriate approach if it is considered within the appropriate evaluation context.

Pluralistic Qualitative Evaluation

Employing pluralistic qualitative approaches to explore how different evaluators and participants make sense of the data provides different ways of understanding data. Considered together, the layers of interpretation can provide an array of perspectives of participants' accounts of their experiences. Considered separately, different interpretations of data can provide views from different dimensions, from which the one(s) of most relevance to the evaluator can be extracted. This can be particularly pertinent when the evaluation involves participants from different aspects of the program, each of whom may have different understandings of the value and purpose of the program and different interests in the outcomes of its evaluation.

Pluralistic use of qualitative methods in the conduct of an evaluation serves to highlight not only convergences but also divergences in the processes and outcomes of the evaluation. When findings do not concur or when they contradict each other, the evaluators are forced to ask why and to return to their choice and use of methods as a starting point to explore further. Qualitative methods do not seek to validate claims about what is true or real, and instead offer a gateway to understanding data and the meanings they hold for those who have supplied it from a range of world-views and belief systems.

In an evaluation context, finding different aspects of the phenomena can be crucial to understanding the impact of a program fully and to informing its future development and application. Whilst offering a form of triangulation, one that values divergence rather than convergence, pluralistic qualitative evaluation can also enhance credibility by its use of different evaluators employing different methods. There is a demand for each evaluator to be accountable for his or her employment of a method and a responsibility to make his or her use of it transparent to the evaluation process. This is best achieved by showing the systematic application of the chosen model of analysis and the adoption of an open reflexive stance that clearly demonstrates how the outcomes are reached through analysis and interpretation. The discussion of the outcomes with fellow evaluators allows for further reflection and accountability and the positioning of the theoretical framework. A team of qualitative evaluators has to work together to agree on the role and status of each method used. Decisions have to be made at the outset of the process about whether the pluralistic use of the qualitative methods is integrative (equal status placed on each) or combined (identification of variables for measurement in a subsequent quantitative study) (Moran-Ellis et al., 2006). It clarifies the ways in which different readings of data are made and the impact of the evaluators and their role on these readings. It makes transparent the pathways the data analysis follows and so provides securely credible qualitative findings.

To illustrate how pluralistic qualitative evaluation can work to both evaluate a program and as an evaluation process, we discuss below a case study of youth participation in a youth inclusion program (Nolas, 2008).

Youth Participation in a Youth Inclusion Program

The Play On program (a pseudonym) is an ongoing national youth inclusion program in England. The policy focus on youth inclusion emerged as a response to growing social exclusion and in particular the number of young people who were not in education, employment, or training (so-called NEETs). Play On operated in 20% of the most deprived areas of England. With similarities to youth-development programs in the United States, the program aimed to reengage young people in education, employment, or training. It did so through the use of a relationship strategy, sporting and other cultural activities, and role models. Unlike diversionary crime-prevention programs, which rely on short-term activities during school breaks, the Play On program operated year round and project workers focused on developing meaningful relationships with young people most at risk of embarking on criminal careers and drug use. With sports and other activities used as hooks, the program worked with young people on a long-term basis, with project workers acting as role models to the young people, supporting young people to turn their lives around and in turn to become role models for other young people in their community. Local projects were often delivered in partnership, with the strategic involvement of youth services, social services, the police, and the volunteer sector.

Beyond the three-pronged program strategy of relationships, sports, and role models, local projects were given the freedom to work with young people in context-appropriate ways, in doing so generating a range of heterogeneous small-scale local projects. These projects often reflected the needs of local communities in inner-city, urban, and rural settings with differences ranging from demographic makeup of the local community to access to facilities and young people's preferences with determined activity provision. The program's departure from established diversionary methods made the program, overall, new and innovative with regard to engaging with socially marginalized young people, breathing fresh air into older, though highly marginalized, practices of youth work (Nolas, in press). Furthermore, the local freedom that each project enjoyed meant that innovation was also rife at a local level, with engagement activities ranging from football to fly fishing and DJ-ing. Finally, the program operated in highly contested space in terms of its focus on young people's inclusion. Young people, more than any other social demographic, raise a number of anxieties for policy makers and practitioners alike. Viewed as either risk makers or risk takers (Sharland, 2006), young people, especially young people who come from chaotic family backgrounds and stigmatized communities of geography and identity, are often caught between punitive and rehabilitative discourses of intervention. The program occupied, and continues to do so, the tricky terrain in an ever-shifting policy landscape that has swung from a preventative to a punitive discourse in the last 15 years (Haw, 2010; Nolas, 2008).

The evaluation study that we make reference to here engaged with many of these features of the Play On program (Humphreys, Nolas, & Olmos, 2006; Nolas, 2008). The evaluators responded to the small-scale nature of the local projects, and the contested nature of the discursive landscape, by designing a fourth-generation evaluation (Guba & Lincoln, 1989) that put young people at the heart of evaluation design. The evaluation was embedded into the everyday life of six local projects by providing young people with participatory video activities, which functioned as an activity, a reflective tool, and a data-gathering strategy. Young people were then supported in making a short 15-minute audiovisual composition reflecting on the key issues in their area, their hopes and aspirations for the future, and the meaning of the Play On program for them. A screening of the audiovisual composition was then held to which other young people and relevant professionals were invited. Focus-group discussions with the young people were organized to explore their interpretations of the short films, and their experience of the evaluation process. At the same time professionals were interviewed formally and informally about their experiences of working with the young people, relevant policy and program documents were analyzed, as was program coverage in local and national print media, and an extensive field-note diary was maintained by the lead researcher over an 18-month period, reflecting on her experience of working with young people in a participative way (Nolas, 2011b). These data were analyzed with the use of a range of analytical strategies. Given her interest in the dynamics of participation, the evaluator drew on constructivist grounded theory (Charmaz, 2006; Emerson, Fretz, & Shaw, 1995) to analyze processes and interactions across the range of data collected. A key feature of the data collected were stories—the stories young people created, the stories they told about their areas, the stories project workers told about the young people, and the stories told about young people in the public sphere through the media and official program documentation. These were analyzed with the use of a narrative analysis framework (Labov & Waletzky, 1967; Parker, 2005). Finally, the material was brought together through a conceptual framework that combined theories of symbolic interactionism (e.g., Mead, 1934), social practice (e.g., de Certeau, 1984), and feminist reflexivity (e.g., Gallop, 2002).

Foregrounding young people's lived experience in the evaluation strategy attempted to give young people a voice and to challenge the binary language of risk makers and risk takers. As such, young people became authors (Humphreys & Brezillon, 2002) of their own experiences, thus intervening in the contested linguistic and practice landscape of youth inclusion. The team's embedding in the local projects, the triangulation of methods, and pluralistic approach to data analysis enabled the evaluators to generate a rich multiperspective picture of young people's lives, their communities, and their participation in the Play On program. This multidimensional understanding of the particularities of the context in which the social intervention was delivered enabled subsequent theory development about the necessary and sufficient conditions under which the program might achieve its aims and objectives. The resulting theory highlighted the temporal dimensions necessary for developing a culture of youth participation (Nolas, in press), the inclusionary *as well as exclusionary* dynamics of such cultures of participation (Nolas, 2011b), and the processes of identification involved in the lived experiences and practices participation (Nolas, 2011a).

Using a pluralistic qualitative approach, however, requires trade-offs. Given its focus on process, experiences, and interactions, the evaluation described above did not carry out any baseline or outcome measurement about young people's achievements of, for example, psychological well-being, belonging, engagement in education, employment, or training, although such data were collected nationally by the program sponsors for auditing and monitoring purposes. The absence of these trends from the research narrative is limiting, because such trends can provide a bigger picture in which to situate the young people's and project workers' experiences. Furthermore, qualitative approaches, and pluralistic qualitative evaluation, might not be appropriate in situations in which more established interventions, with well-developed program theories, are being delivered to familiar stakeholders, in familiar contexts (e.g., the third or fourth cycle of a well-established parenting program in the same community, assuming parents experience similar difficulties as those of previous cycles). Rapid-response evaluations that do not allow the time for in-depth qualitative data collection and analysis would also make pluralistic qualitative evaluation unsuitable. Nevertheless, we would argue that although it may not be possible to operationalize full-blown pluralistic qualitative evaluation (PQE), a PQE mindset could serve as a useful heuristic and reminder, in any evaluation context, of the multiple and overlapping ways in which social reality is constructed.

Discussion

The example above illustrates how adopting a pluralistic qualitative approach to evaluation can enable rigorous small-scale, social-change evaluation. Through inclusion of the stakeholders alongside the reflexive input of the evaluator(s), this approach constitutes an inherent accountability and transparency. By combining worldviews brought by different qualitative methods and participants, space is made for divergent meanings to be surfaced in the data and different methodological perspectives to be brought to its interpretation. Different audience interests in process, salience, appropriateness, and satisfaction (Hansen & Rieper, 2009) are represented in outcomes that can be considered separately or combined to provide a more holistic view of the evaluation. By including a number of evaluators, as is often needed to ensure sufficient expertise in each method, complex research can be conducted, which arguably better represents the complexity of the social processes under evaluation.

The pluralistic qualitative approach resonates with the principles of transformative evaluation (Mertens, 2009), itself an antecedent of fourth-generation evaluation (Guba & Lincoln, 1989). This responsive, constructivist approach to evaluation develops through processes of iteration to access individual and group constructions of meanings of issues, claims, and concerns. Differences are addressed through evaluator-led processes of negotiation with the stakeholders. Fourth-generation evaluation assumes no certain truth and instead seeks to incorporate the range of worldviews brought by the stakeholders and evaluators to the project. Through a rigorous and accountable process of combining qualitative methods, the process becomes capable of flexing with meanings and perspectives brought to and emerging from the data. It does not seek to converge on one explanation. Thus this approach incorporates the issues, claims, and concerns of all the stakeholders and promotes a process that holds multiple worldviews and belief systems at its center.

With its focus on gaining more understanding of social processes and interactions, critical behavioral science recognizes the value of weaving qualitative methodologies into mixed-methods evaluation (Hesse-Biber, 2012). A pluralistic qualitative approach extends the range of an evaluation by providing a methodological framework for systematically analyzing different stakeholders' perspectives. Importantly, PQE enables and tolerates these different perspectives and asks what can be learned from the tensions of difference. As program designers and evaluators alike seek to understand the complexity of human experience and action better, pluralistic qualitatively driven perspectives in mixed-methods approaches to evaluation offer a new theoretical lens for organizing these sense-making processes.

References

Cartwright, N., & Munro, E. (2010). The limitations of randomized controlled trials in predicting effectiveness. *Evaluation in Clinical Practice, 16,* 260–266.

Charmaz, K. (2006). *Constructing grounded theory: A practical guide through qualitative analysis.* London, England: Sage.

de Certeau, M. (1984). *The practice of everyday life.* Berkeley, CA: University of California Press.

Emerson, P., & Frosh, S. (2004). *Critical narrative analysis in psychology.* Basingstoke, England: Palgrave Macmillan.

Emerson, R. M., Fretz, R. I., & Shaw, L. L. (1995). *Writing ethnographic field notes.* Chicago, IL: University of Chicago Press.

Frost, N. A. (2009). "Do you know what I mean?": The use of a pluralistic narrative analysis approach in the interpretation of an interview. *Qualitative Research, 9*(1), 9–29.

Gallop, J. (2002). *Anecdotal theory.* Durham, NC: Duke University Press.

Guba, E. G., & Lincoln, Y. S. (1989). *Fourth generation evaluation.* Beverly Hills, CA: Sage.

Hansen, H. F., & Rieper, O. (2009). The evidence movement: The development and consequences of methodologies in review practices. *Evaluation 15*(2), 141–163.

Haw, K. (2010). Risk and resilience: The ordinary and extraordinary everyday lives of young people living in a high crime area. *Youth & Society, 41*(4), 451–474.

Hesse-Biber, S. N. (2012). Weaving a multimethodology and mixed methods praxis into randomized control trials to enhance credibility. *Qualitative Inquiry, 18*(10), 876–889.

Humphreys, P., & Brezillon, P. (2002). Combining rich and restricted languages in multimedia: Enrichment of context for innovative decisions. In F. Adam, P. Brezillon, P. Humphreys, & J.-C. Pomerol (Eds.), *Decision making and decision support in the internet age* (pp. 695–708). Cork, Ireland: Oaktree Press.

Humphreys, P., Nolas, S.-M., & Olmos, G. (2006, April 28). *Positive futures young people's views project final report: Integrated findings on young people's views.* The London multimedia laboratory for audio visual composition and communication. Retrieved from http://www.lml.lse.ac.uk

Labov, W., & Waletzky, J. (1967). Narrative analysis: Oral versions of personal experience. In J. Helm (Ed.), *Essays on the verbal and visual arts.* Seattle, WA: University of Washington Press.

Mason, J. (2006). Mixing methods in a qualitatively driven way. *Qualitative Research, 6*(1), 9–26.

Mead, G. H. (1934). *Mind, self and society from the standpoint of a social behaviourist*. Chicago, IL: University of Chicago Press.

Mertens, D. M. (2009). *Transformative research and evaluation*. New York, NY: Guilford.

Moran-Ellis, J., Alexander, V. D., Cronin, A., Dickinson, M., Fielding, J., Sleney, J., & Thomas, H. (2006). Triangulation and integration: Processes, claims and implications. *Qualitative Research, 6*(1), 45–59.

Mosse, D. (2005) *Cultivating development: Ethnography of aid policy and practice*. London, England: Pluto Press.

Nolas, S.-M. (2008). *Disrupting the emancipatory narrative: An ethnographic study of participation in a youth inclusion programme* (Unpublished doctoral dissertation). London School of Economics and Political Sciences, London, England.

Nolas, S.-M. (2011a). Stories as indicators of practical knowledge: Analysing project workers' talk from a study of participation in a youth inclusion programme. *Journal of Community and Applied Social Psychology, 21*(2), 138–150.

Nolas, S.-M. (2011b). Reflections on the enactment of children's participation rights through research: Between relational and transactional spaces. *Children and Youth Services Review, 33*(7), 1196–1202.

Nolas, S.-M. (in press). Exploring young people's and youth workers' experiences of spaces of youth development: Creating cultures of participation. *Journal of Youth Studies*. doi:10.1080/13676261.2013.793789

Parker, I. (2005). *Qualitative psychology: Introducing radical research*. New York, NY: Open University Press.

Petticrew, M., & Roberts, H. (2003). Evidence, hierarchies, and typologies: Horses for courses. *Journal of Epidemiology and Community Health, 57*, 527–529.

Petticrew, M., & Roberts, H. (2006). *Systematic reviews in the social sciences: A practical guide*. Oxford, England: Blackwell.

Pressman, J. L., & Wildavsky, A. (1973). *Implementation* (3rd ed.). London, England: California Press.

Robson, C. (2002). *Real world research* (2nd ed.). Oxford, England: Blackwell.

Sharland, E. (2006). Young people, risk taking and risk making: Some thoughts for social work. *British Journal of Social Work, 26*, 247–265.

NOLLAIG FROST is a senior lecturer in psychology at the Department of Psychology, Middlesex University, United Kingdom.

SEVASTI-MELISSA NOLAS is a lecturer in social work in the Department of Social Work & Social Care, University of Sussex, United Kingdom.

NEW DIRECTIONS FOR EVALUATION • DOI: 10.1002/ev

Collins, K. M. T., & Onwuegbuzie, A. J. (2013). Establishing interpretive consistency when mixing approaches: Role of sampling designs in evaluations. In D. M. Mertens & S. Hesse-Biber (Eds.), *Mixed methods and credibility of evidence in evaluation. New Directions for Evaluation, 138*, 85–95.

8

Establishing Interpretive Consistency When Mixing Approaches: Role of Sampling Designs in Evaluations

Kathleen M. T. Collins, Anthony J. Onwuegbuzie

Abstract

The goal of this chapter is to recommend quality criteria to guide evaluators' selections of sampling designs when mixing approaches. First, we contextualize our discussion of quality criteria and sampling designs by discussing the concept of interpretive consistency and how it impacts sampling decisions. Embedded in this discussion are challenges impacting interpretive consistency. Strategies and an integrative sampling framework comprising published frameworks are presented to facilitate evaluators' decisions about selecting sampling designs in accordance to specific criteria. We conclude by presenting an illustrative application of mixed sampling design criteria to a published mixed evaluation study as a heuristic example of a way of embedding sampling criteria in a mixed evaluation. ©Wiley Periodicals, Inc., and the American Evaluation Association.

Establishing credibility of evidence requires evaluators to devise, to apply, and to evaluate quality criteria at varying stages of the inquiry process, namely, the conceptualization, design, implementation, and utilization stages. Implementing quality criteria at multiple junctures within an evaluation is an iterative, interactive, and dynamic process that ultimately elevates the transparency of the inquiry process. Mixed methods research, hereafter referred to as mixed research, allows the evaluator to implement a combination of qualitative and quantitative approaches, thereby optimizing the opportunities to acquire credible evidence. *Mixed research* is the preferred term because mixed methods research is not just about methods and data. Mixed research also is very much about philosophy and values. In program evaluation studies, a mixed approach can be an effective approach toward conducting multipurpose evaluations involving formative and summative processes designed to assess impact evaluations, and toward promoting "synergistic understanding" of interpretation of outcomes and inputs (Bamberger, Rao, & Woolcock, 2010; Sammons, 2010, p. 698). Bamberger et al. (2010) outline specific contexts that are applicable—particularly for mixed designs, such as implementing monitoring systems, expanding data sets to include contextual factors, and identifying potential variables that could contribute to stronger statistical analyses. Sammons (2010) observes that a mixed inquiry has the potential to promote collaboration among groups of evaluators who tend to emphasize evidence that favors one approach in contrast to the other approach (e.g., school improvement evaluators [QUAL] and school effectiveness evaluators [QUAN]). Integral to the effective utilization of a mixed inquiry in conducting evaluations is selecting sampling designs for both approaches, and implementing strategies to identify the samples of interest. This chapter is designed to outline explicit ways that evaluators can improve their sampling designs and make transparent the design process within a mixed inquiry, thereby enhancing the link between evidence and credibility when formulating conclusions and inferences.

Interpretive Consistency

Sampling designs comprise the selection of sampling schemes—purposive and/or random—accompanied by the selection of a sample size, subsample size, or group size per approach, and these designs have multifaceted implications. When utilizing a mixed research approach, these sample design decisions elevate in complexity because sampling decisions influence the degree to which the evaluator can achieve consistency between the sampling designs and the conclusions, inferences, generalizations, and transferability of findings—an outcome known as interpretive consistency (Collins, Onwuegbuzie, & Jiao, 2006, 2007)—thereby enhancing research utilization.

To facilitate interpretive consistency, Collins (2010) developed an integrative typology comprising attributes of selective sampling frameworks. Integrative aspects of the typology accommodate the emergent characteristic of a mixed evaluation that might have multiple phases and different sampling designs per phase. Each dimension of the typology is an aspect of published sampling frameworks (i.e., Kemper, Stringfield, & Teddlie, 2003; Onwuegbuzie & Collins, 2007; Teddlie & Yu, 2007), and different types of

Table 8.1. Description of Collins's (2010) Integrative Typology

Criteria	Description
Criterion 1	Relationship between the samples per approach and the time orientation of the approaches
Time orientation of the approaches	Concurrent orientation Implementation of each approach is independent. Integration of findings occurs at the implementation stage, when the researcher is forming interpretations and conclusions Sequential Orientation Dependent relationship exists between the two approaches when utilizing a sequential design. In this case, the decisions pertaining to the design and implementation of one approach are influenced by the decisions pertaining to the other approach
Criterion 2	Relationship between the quantitative and qualitative samples
Identical sample	Same participants comprise the sample participating in each approach
Parallel sample	Sample participants are different but selection criterion requires that each sample represent the same population
Nested sample	Sample participants participating in one approach represent a subsample of participants comprising the sample participating in the other approach
Multilevel sample	Samples participating in each approach are different; however, each sample represents a hierarchical relationship with the topic under investigation
Criterion 3	Relationship between the compilation of selected sampling schemes and the type of generalization/transference guiding the design
Type of generalization	Statistical Naturalistic Analytic Case-to-case transfer
Criterion 4 Type of data collected	Relationship between the types of data collected Qualitative data only Quantitative data only Combination of both data types
Criterion 5 Emphasis of approach	Relationship between emphasis placed on each approach when forming inferences and generalizations Dominant Dominant-less Approximately equal
For more information see Collins (2010)	

generalizations and transferences (i.e., Curtis, Gesler, Smith, & Washburn, 2000; Firestone, 1993; Kennedy, 1979; Miles & Huberman, 1994; Stake, 2005). Subsequently, the crafting of this integrative framework embodies a systemic approach; this is an approach that is recommended by critics who view utilization of a single typology as being too restrictive given the diversity of mixed designs and the emergent characteristic of a mixed inquiry (Hall & Howard, 2008; Teddlie & Tashakkori, 2009). Table 8.1, adapted from Collins (2010), identifies the typology's dimensions.

Challenges Affecting Interpretive Consistency

Achieving interpretive consistency involves the evaluator addressing a series of distinct yet interrelated challenges—unique to mixing approaches that can compromise interpretive consistency—unless addressed by a strategy. The first challenge, representation, reflects the degree that the samples selected (a) are representative of the population of interest (quantitative sample[s]), and (b) provide information-rich cases (qualitative sample[s]). The evaluator's decisions pertaining to the selection of cases via sampling schemes can impact the degree to which theoretical validity is attained in terms of the evaluator formulating logical and appropriate transferences and formulating generalizations to the underlying population. Collecting and integrating both forms of data within a mixed inquiry allows the evaluator to obtain *empirical precision* (quantitative data) and *descriptive precision* (qualitative data) (Onwuegbuzie, 2003, p. 396 [italics in the original]). Prebriefing, an interview technique recommended by Collins, Onwuegbuzie, and Sutton (2006) could be implemented, whereby the evaluator would develop a set of questions and interview the participants before the evaluation commences. Implementing this technique would allow the evaluator to assess the sample characteristics relative to the inquiry's goal. Doing so can narrow the sample's extraneous characteristics and facilitate the evaluator's efforts to assess cases most pertinent toward addressing the inquiry's goal. Furthermore, a homogeneous sample reduces the number of cases necessary to achieve data saturation (i.e., occurring when information occurs so repeatedly that the evaluator can anticipate it and whereby the collection of more data appears to have no additional interpretive worth; Sandelowski, 2008; Saumure & Given, 2008) or theoretical saturation (i.e., occurring when the evaluator can assume that her/his emergent theory is developed adequately to fit any future data collected; Sandelowski, 2008), and reduces the number of sampling units necessary to detect statistically significant relationships and differences (Guest, Bunce, & Johnson, 2006).

Another commonly used strategy to achieve empirical precision is a power analysis. This term defines a process of analysis implemented to ascertain the number of participants necessary to detect statistically significant differences or relationships at a nominal level of statistical significance (e.g., 0.05) at a specified effect size (e.g., moderate effect size) and power (e.g., 0.80)—assuming these differences or relationships exist in the underlying population. This type of power analysis is referred to as an a priori power analysis. Evaluators also should consider conducting a post-hoc power analysis (Onwuegbuzie & Leech, 2004), especially when the difference or relationship examined is not statistically significant. Another strategy is to maximize descriptive validity (i.e., factual accuracy of the account as documented by the evaluator; Maxwell, 1992) by employing member checking not only to validate the accuracy of the evaluator's account or text, but also to give the participant the opportunity to revise and/or to expand on responses made in the previous interview(s), which enhances descriptive precision (Onwuegbuzie, 2003), and, subsequently, provides an audit trail—accumulating evidence and establishing credibility of conclusions. Member checking also could balance the emic perspectives of the participants and the etic perspective of the evaluator in terms of the veracity of the conclusions and generalizations, thereby enhancing the ability for readers to make naturalistic generalizations (i.e., the degree that the conclusions resonate as important to the stakeholders; Stake, 2005). The "representativeness/saturation trade-off" proposed by Teddlie and Tashakkori (2009, p. 184) is a strategy applicable for addressing interpretive inconsistency arising from utilizing different sampling units or cases of varying sizes in both approaches. The trade-off reflects the evaluator's decision to place more emphasis on one approach in drawing conclusions in contrast to the other approach, thereby limiting the representativeness of the quantitative sample or limiting theoretical saturation—as a consequence of this decision.

Sampling designs impact the challenges of legitimation and integration, specifically the following three legitimation types identified by Onwuegbuzie and Johnson (2006): sample integration, weakness minimization, and conversion. Implicit in the process of addressing these forms of legitimation are the type of question or set of questions addressed in the evaluation, the degree that the evaluator has incorporated a systemic form of validation throughout the evaluation, and the evaluator's philosophical proclivities in terms of determining what constitutes credible data, and what are the appropriate data-collection techniques (Collins, Onwuegbuzie, & Johnson, 2012). Sample integration legitimation reflects the extent to which the relationship between the quantitative and qualitative samples permits the evaluator to draw appropriate meta-inferences, generalizations, and transference. Unless an identical sample (i.e., the same participants participate in both approaches) is utilized across both phases, sample integration is compromised unless the evaluator places more emphasis on one set of findings when drawing conclusions and meta-inferences, and makes this decision transparent in the reporting of the findings. This decision is influenced by the type and number of generalizations desired by the evaluator based on the purpose of the evaluation. For example, an evaluator might desire to make an external statistical generalization (i.e., making generalizations, predictions, or inferences on data yielded from a representative statistical [i.e., optimally random and large] sample to the population from which the sample was drawn); cf. Onwuegbuzie, Slate, Leech, & Collins, 2009 for findings stemming from the quantitative phase(s) and an analytic generalization (i.e., "applied to wider theory on the basis of how selected cases 'fit' with general constructs"; Curtis et al., 2000, p. 1002) for findings stemming from the qualitative phase(s). The challenge then would be to select an appropriate sampling design that justifies both sets of generalizations and allows any ensuing meta-inferences to incorporate both sets of generalizations.

Weakness minimization legitimation reflects the degree that weaknesses or limitations associated with one approach are compensated by the strengths associated with the other approach. The type of sampling schemes accompanied by the size of the samples impacts the degree to which both approaches in tandem can attain the evidence necessary to address the study's goal, objective, and research question. This issue of attaining the necessary amount of data is exacerbated when one type of data (e.g., qualitative) is converted or transformed to the other data type (e.g., quantitative) in a process known as quantitizing (i.e., converting or transforming qualitative data into numerical codes that can be analyzed statistically; Miles & Huberman, 1994; Tashakkori & Teddlie, 1998) or qualitizing (i.e., converting or transforming quantitative data into qualitative data that can be analyzed qualitatively; Tashakkori & Teddlie, 1998). These conversions of data are undertaken for the purpose of complementarity (i.e., seeking elaboration, illustration, enhancement, and clarification of the results from one method with findings from the other method; Greene, Caracelli, & Graham, 1989), development (i.e., using the results from one method to help inform the other method; Greene et al., 1989), and/or expansion (i.e., expanding the breadth and range of a study by using multiple methods for different study phases; Greene et al., 1989)—all of which lead to an enhancement in the interpretation of the initial data collected (quantitative or qualitative).

Q methodology and Q factor analysis as a methodology and a multivariate technique, respectively, can be used to enhance interpretations of qualitative data collected (Newman & Ramlo, 2010). When quantitizing qualitative data, the sample size pertaining to the number of cases can impact the degree to which the data set can be analyzed with the use of these advanced multivariate techniques, and other techniques such as correspondence analysis (for an example, see Onwuegbuzie, Frels, Leech, & Collins, 2011) and chi-squared automatic interaction detection (for an example, see Onwuegbuzie & Collins, 2010). Deployment of these techniques would allow the evaluator to obtain a multidimensional interpretation of the data, thereby enhancing the opportunity to assess different facets of the research question.

The challenges pertaining to politics and ethics represent the most far-reaching impact because the decisions pertinent to data collection, interpretation, and generalization of the findings (e.g., naturalistic general-ization) involve a full range of stakeholders, including the client and other relevant stakeholders in the public domain. Collins et al. (2012) define the challenges of politics and ethics as reflecting "the degree that the conclu-sions represent a balanced and socially ethical perspective and are recog-nized as viable and useful to the multiple stakeholders, such as social groups and funding agencies impacted by the inquiry" (p. 852). Addressing these challenges affects political legitimation, which is the degree that the evaluator identifies the interests, values, and viewpoints of a range of stake-holders or intended users when conducting an evaluation and interpreting results (Onwuegbuzie & Johnson, 2006). These challenges resonate with the Integrity/Honesty component of the American Evaluation Association's (2004) *Guiding Principles for Educators.*

Sampling in terms of identifying the cases and sampling units impacts these challenges, and two strategies, prebriefing and debriefing, can facil-itate evaluators' sampling decisions. Prebriefing participants prior to the commencement of the data-collection activities of the evaluation and debriefing participants at the evaluation's conclusion can facilitate evalua-tors' efforts to address this form of legitimation. Also, aligned to political legitimation is inside–outside legitimation (Onwuegbuzie & Johnson, 2006), whereby the evaluator balances both the insiders' (e.g., client) views and outsiders' (relevant stakeholders in the public domain) views when interpreting (e.g., description, explanation) the findings. Further, it is important for evaluators to be aware of biases that might mitigate this process. Subsequently, the evaluator could be interviewed to ascertain her or his perceptions of the evaluation process, as a whole, and the evalua-tor's perceptions of the samples, in particular. The following debriefing topics are related to potential biases and could compromise political legit-imation: evaluator's background, perceptions of the participants, interpre-tations of the evaluation's findings, unexpected issues that occur in the evaluation, and the evaluator's response to these issues (Onwuegbuzie, Leech, & Collins, 2008). Illuminating evaluators' awareness relative to these topics elevates the degree to which the evaluators can address polit-ical legitimation and the challenge of politics. Additionally, these strate-gies have the potential to obtain information that can serve to identify the stakeholders' ethical values. As noted by Johnson (2011), evaluators who "concurrently and equally value multiple perspectives and paradigms" (p. 4) in particular "*should dialectically listen to multiple ethical values that might be relevant to the research*" (p. 10) [emphasis in original]. Nowhere in the evaluation process is this more relevant than at the sampling stage, wherein sampling strategies pertaining to the quantitative and qualitative phases are combined or integrated into a unified and coherent mixed sam-pling design.

As surmised by Onwuegbuzie and Collins (2007), regardless of the sam-pling design used, all sample members receive maximum protection and every attempt is made to do no harm. Maintaining an ethical sampling design also means that evaluators should "continually evaluate their sampling designs and procedures for ethical and scientific appropriateness throughout the course of their studies" (Onwuegbuzie & Collins, 2007, p. 306).

Application of Sampling Criteria: Heuristic Example

The sampling decisions in the study outlined below are critiqued to illustrate how the strategies presented above and the dimensions of the integrative framework (Collins, 2010) could be embedded within a mixed evaluation program. Abildso, Zizzi, Gilleland, Thomas, and Bonner (2010) examined the outcomes in terms of physical and psychosocial impact of a 12-week cognitive-behavioral weight-management program. Abildso et al. implemented a sequential design with nested samples. Data obtained in the quantitative phase ($n = 55$) were used to stratify the sample members into groups, and the qualitative sample ($n = 11$) represented a subgroup of the larger sample. Two types of data were collected. Quantitative data comprised numbers measuring participants' physical responses to the program, and their psychosocial outcomes were measured via responses to questionnaires. Transcribed interview transcripts comprised the qualitative data. Although not stated specifically by the authors, it appeared that the quantitative data were given the most weight based on the following statement: "the qualitative data provided additional depth of understanding to the quantitative outcomes" (p. 290). Limitations pertaining to the lack of a control group and the relatively small sample size were specified, and the authors noted the following: ". . . generalizability of the findings is limited to individuals that (a) are similar in socio-demographic characteristics, (b) are insured, and (c) have access to the unique features of this WMP [weight management program]" (p. 291). Although the authors did not specify the type of generalization (e.g., statistical, naturalistic, analytic, case-to-case), it appears that the authors were referring to a case-to-case transfer (Firestone, 1993; Kennedy, 1979), such that the generalization was not statistical but referred to conceptual power (Miles & Huberman, 1994). In terms of applying sampling criteria noted above, the evaluators who conducted the interviews could be debriefed by being interviewed by a peer not associated directly with the program evaluation (Onwuegbuzie et al., 2008). The interview could prompt evaluators' reflexivity and add another level of qualitative analysis, in terms of identifying potential bias in data interpretation and adding potentially new insights in data interpretation, which could allow for a further integration of findings.

Conclusions

The application of sampling criteria to a heuristic example demonstrated that adhering to criteria presented in this chapter and outlined in the table could enhance the transparency of evaluators' decisions. For example, Abildso et al. (2010) did not state explicitly the emphasis of approach that they implemented when formulating their conclusions, and they did not specify explicitly the type of generalization that the data source permitted given the limitations in terms of sample size and design considerations. The lack of explicit statements can compromise the transparency of the process of conducting a mixed evaluation, and compromise potentially the degree to which stakeholders perceive the findings to be legitimate, and the degree to which other evaluators can replicate the methodology.

Even if quality, appropriateness, meaningfulness, and utility of the underlying question(s) are optimal, a poor sampling design would invalidate the evaluation's findings and lead to interpretive inconsistency that, in turn, would lead to meta-inferences that lack credibility. As we have shown in this chapter, interpretive consistency is impacted by five distinct yet interrelated challenges: representation, legitimation, integration, politics, and ethics. Guidelines in the forms of strategies and an integrative sampling framework were presented. These guidelines were accompanied by an illustrative application to a published mixed evaluation. We hope that this chapter provides a resource for evaluators, and we encourage other evaluators and methodologists to continue work in this area.

References

Abildso, C., Zizzi, S., Gilleland, D., Thomas, J., & Bonner, D. (2010). A mixed methods evaluation of a 12-week insurance-sponsored weight management program incorporating cognitive-behavioral counseling. *Journal of Mixed Methods Research, 4,* 278–294. doi:10.1177/1558689810376949

American Evaluation Association. (2004). *Guiding principle for evaluators.* Retrieved from http.eval.org/Publications/Guiding Principles.asp

Bamberger, M., Rao, V., & Woolcock, M. (2010). Using mixed methods in monitoring and evaluation: Experiences from international development. In A. Tashakkori & C. Teddlie (Eds.), *Sage handbook of mixed methods in social and behavioral research* (2nd ed., pp. 613–641). Thousand Oaks, CA: Sage.

Collins, K. M. T. (2010). Advanced sampling designs in integrated research: Current practices and emerging trends in the social and behavioral sciences. In A. Tashakkori & C. Teddlie (Eds.), *Sage handbook of mixed methods in social and behavioral research* (2nd ed., pp. 353–377). Thousand Oaks, CA: Sage.

Collins, K. M. T., Onwuegbuzie, A. J., & Jiao, Q. G. (2006). Prevalence of mixed methods sampling designs in social science research. *Evaluation and Research in Education, 19,* 83–101. doi:10.2167/eri421.0

Collins, K. M. T., Onwuegbuzie, A. J., & Jiao, Q. G. (2007). A mixed methods investigation of mixed methods sampling designs in social and health sciences research. *Journal of Mixed Methods Research, 1,* 267–294. doi:10.1177/1558689807299526

Collins, K. M. T., Onwuegbuzie, A. J., & Johnson, R. B. (2012). Securing a place at the table: Introducing legitimation criteria for the conduct of mixed research. *American Behavioral Scientist, 56,* 849–865. doi:10.1177/0002764211433799

Collins, K. M. T., Onwuegbuzie, A. J., & Sutton, I. L. (2006). A model incorporating the rationale and purpose for conducting mixed methods research in special education and beyond. *Learning Disabilities: A Contemporary Journal, 4,* 67–100.

Curtis, S., Gesler, W., Smith, G., & Washburn, S. (2000). Approaches to sampling and case selection in qualitative research: Examples in the geography of health. *Social Science and Medicine, 50,* 1001–1014. doi:10.1016/S0277-9536(99)00350-0

Firestone, W. A. (1993). Alternate arguments for generalizing from data, as applied to qualitative research. *Educational Researcher, 2*(4), 16–23. doi:10.2307/1177100

Greene, J. C., Caracelli, V. J., & Graham, W. F. (1989). Toward a conceptual framework for mixed-method evaluation designs. *Educational Evaluation and Policy Analysis, 11,* 255–274. doi:10.3102/01623737011003255

Guest, G., Bunce, A., & Johnson, L. (2006). How many interviews are enough? An experiment with data saturation and variability. *Field Methods, 18*(1), 59–82. doi:10.1177/1525822X05279903

Hall, B., & Howard, K. (2008). A synergistic approach: Conducting mixed methods research with typological and systemic design considerations. *Journal of Mixed Methods Research, 2,* 248–269. doi:10.1177/1558689808314622

Johnson, R. B. (2011, May). *Dialectical pluralism: A metaparadigm to help us hear and "combine" our valued differences.* Paper presented at the Seventh International Congress of Qualitative Inquiry, Champaign, IL.

Kemper, E. A., Stringfield, S., & Teddlie, C. (2003). Mixed methods sampling strategies in social science research. In A. Tashakkori & C. Teddlie (Eds.), *Handbook of mixed methods in social and behavioral research* (pp. 273–296). Thousand Oaks, CA: Sage.

Kennedy, M. (1979). Generalizing from single case studies. *Evaluation Quarterly, 3,* 661–678. doi:10.1177/0193841X7900300409

Maxwell, J. A. (1992). Understanding and validity in qualitative research. *Harvard Educational Review, 62,* 279–299.

Miles, M. A., & Huberman, A. M. (1994). *Qualitative data analysis: An expanded sourcebook* (2nd ed.). Thousand Oaks, CA: Sage.

Newman, I., & Ramlo, S. (2010). Using Q methodology and Q factor analysis in mixed methods research. In A. Tashakkori & C. Teddlie (Eds.), *Sage handbook of mixed methods in social and behavioral research* (2nd ed., pp. 505–530). Thousand Oaks, CA: Sage.

Onwuegbuzie, A. J. (2003). Effect sizes in qualitative research: A prolegomenon. *Quality & Quantity: International Journal of Methodology, 37,* 393–409. doi:10.1023/A: 1027379223537

Onwuegbuzie, A. J., & Collins, K. M. T. (2007). A typology of mixed methods sampling designs in social science research. *The Qualitative Report, 12,* 281–316. Retrieved from http://www.nova.edu/ssss/QR/QR12-2/onwuegbuzie2.pdf

Onwuegbuzie, A. J., & Collins, K. M. T. (2010). An innovative method for stress and coping researchers for analyzing themes in mixed research: Introducing chi-square automatic interaction detection (CHAID). In G. S. Gates, W. H. Gmelch, & M. Wolverton (Series Eds.) and K. M. T. Collins, A. J. Onwuegbuzie, & Q. G. Jiao (Vol. Eds.), *The Research on Stress and Coping in Education Series: Vol. 5. Toward a broader understanding of stress and coping: Mixed methods approaches* (pp. 287–301). Charlotte, NC: Information Age.

Onwuegbuzie, A. J., Frels, R. K., Leech, N. L., & Collins, K. M. T. (2011). A mixed research study of pedagogical approaches and student learning in doctoral-level mixed research courses. *International Journal of Multiple Research Approaches, 5,* 169–199. doi:10.5172/mra.2011.5.2.169

Onwuegbuzie, A. J., & Johnson, R. B. (2006). The validity issue in mixed research. *Research in the Schools, 13*(1), 48–63.

Onwuegbuzie, A. J., & Leech, N. L. (2004). Post-hoc power: A concept whose time has come. *Understanding Statistics, 3,* 201–230. doi:10.1207/s15328031us0304_1

Onwuegbuzie, A. J., Leech, N. L., & Collins, K. M. T. (2008). Interviewing the interpretive researcher: A method for addressing the crises of representation, legitimation, and praxis. *International Journal of Qualitative Methods, 7*(4), 1–17. Retrieved from https://ejournals.library.ualberta.ca/index.php/IJQM/article/view/1701/3818

Onwuegbuzie, A. J., Slate, J. R., Leech, N. L., & Collins, K. M. T. (2009). Mixed data analysis: Advanced integration techniques. *International Journal of Multiple Research Approaches, 3,* 13–33. doi:10.5172/mra.455.3.1.13

Sammons, P. (2010). The contribution of mixed methods to recent research on educational effectiveness. In A. Tashakkori & C. Teddlie (Eds.), *Sage handbook of mixed methods in social and behavioral research* (2nd ed., pp. 697–723). Thousand Oaks, CA: Sage.

Sandelowski, M. (2008). Theoretical saturation. In L. M. Given (Ed.), *The Sage encyclopedia of qualitative methods* (Vol. 1, pp. 875–876). Thousand Oaks, CA: Sage.

Saumure, K., & Given, L. M. (2008). Data saturation. In L. M. Given (Ed.), *The Sage encyclopedia of qualitative methods* (Vol. 1, pp. 195–196). Thousand Oaks, CA: Sage.

Stake, R. E. (2005). Qualitative case studies. In N. K. Denzin & Y. S. Lincoln (Eds.), *The Sage handbook of qualitative research* (3rd ed., pp. 443–466). Thousand Oaks, CA: Sage.

Tashakkori, A., & Teddlie, C. (1998). *Mixed methodology: Combining qualitative and quantitative approaches* (Applied Social Research Methods Series, Vol. 46). Thousand Oaks, CA: Sage.

Teddlie, C., & Tashakkori, A. (2009). *Foundations of mixed methods research: Integrating quantitative and qualitative approaches in the social and   behavioral sciences.* Thousand Oaks, CA: Sage.

Teddlie, C., & Yu, F. (2007). Mixed methods sampling: A typology with examples. *Journal of Mixed Methods Research, 1,* 77–100. doi:10.1177/2345678906292430

KATHLEEN M. T. COLLINS *is a professor at the University of Arkansas at Fayetteville.*

ANTHONY J. ONWUEGBUZIE *is a professor at Sam Houston State University.*

Caracelli, V. J., & Cooksy, L. J. (2013). Incorporating qualitative evidence in systematic reviews: Strategies and challenges. In D. M. Mertens & S. Hesse-Biber (Eds.), *Mixed methods and credibility of evidence in evaluation. New Directions for Evaluation, 138,* 97–108.

9

Incorporating Qualitative Evidence in Systematic Reviews: Strategies and Challenges

Valerie J. Caracelli, Leslie J. Cooksy

Abstract

The quality of mixed methods systematic reviews relies on the quality of primary-level studies. The synthesis of qualitative evidence and the recent development of synthesizing mixed methods studies hold promise, but also pose challenges to evidence synthesis. ©Wiley Periodicals, Inc., and the American Evaluation Association.

Over the past decade, U.S. federal agencies have faced increasing demands to focus funds on interventions with rigorous evidence of effectiveness. The increased emphasis on accountability in the United States has fueled the growth of evidence-based practice reviews (U.S. Government Accountability Office [GAO], 2009; Zief & Agodini, 2012). This growth in systematic reviews is evidenced abroad as well (Hansen & Rieper, 2009). Although many reviews are focused on effectiveness, the refrain "what works" is not the only one of interest to policy makers. For example, at GAO, evaluation synthesis serves as a systematic procedure

---

The views expressed in this chapter do not represent the policy or position of the U.S. Government Accountability Office.

NEW DIRECTIONS FOR EVALUATION, no. 138, Summer 2013 © Wiley Periodicals, Inc., and the American Evaluation Association. Published online in Wiley Online Library (wileyonlinelibrary.com) • DOI: 10.1002/ev.20061

for organizing findings from existing studies, assessing them, and using them as a database to answer specific kinds of questions (e.g., GAO, 1992a, 1992b, 2012). Over the years, the agency has brought evidence to bear on value-laden topics, such as racial disparities in death penalty sentencing, the cycle of sexual abuse, and school vouchers, among others. In addition to informing policy makers, systematic reviews provide knowledge to providers of services who want to know what is known about a particular topic, or whether an intervention may prove beneficial to particular clients in particular contexts.

Labin (2008), in Smith and Brandon's *Fundamental Issues in Evaluation*, provides a historical overview of evaluation synthesis from a traditional literature review to systematic evaluation synthesis. Analytic strategies include meta-analysis, a range of methods for synthesizing qualitative research (Barnett-Page & Thomas, 2009), and, more recently, mixed methods approaches (Pope, Mays, & Popay, 2007). A benefit of evaluation synthesis is that evidence from multiple studies, assessed for sound methodology, can provide greater support for a finding than evidence from a single study. The Cochrane Collaboration (http://www.cochrane.org) established in 1993 and the Campbell Collaboration (http://www.campbell-collaboration.org) established in 1999 are the forerunners, and are among the most well-known entities conducting evidence reviews. In 2009, GAO reviewed six federally supported systematic review initiatives and the steps each took to assess the quality of evaluation evidence, synthesize evidence, and draw conclusions about intervention effectiveness.

Review initiatives focused on effectiveness vary on the kinds of evidence they include. For example, some screen out all but randomized controlled trials (e.g., Coalition for Evidence Based Policy's Top Tier Initiative, http://toptierevidence.org); others include both randomized and quasi-experimental designs (e.g., the Department of Education's What Works Clearinghouse, http://ies.ed.gov/ncee/wwc; and some include observational studies (e.g., the Agency for Health Research and Quality's [AHRQ] evidence-based practice centers [EPCs], http://www.effectivehealthcare.ahrq.gov). Restricting reviews to experimental designs reflects a goal of ruling out alternative explanations for evidence of program effects. Although these designs may be an appropriate emphasis for the "what works" goal, it has long been recognized that experimental and quasi-experimental designs are considerably strengthened by the inclusion of qualitative information (Rossi, Lipsey, & Freeman, 2004). Ethnographic studies in conjunction with experimental designs have been shown to increase accuracy, provide important information about context, and enhance explanation and confidence in findings (Caracelli, 2006; GAO, 2003).

Thus, although systematic reviews, especially those focused on effectiveness, often give priority to experimental designs and quantitative information, systematic reviews can also be based solely on qualitative evidence or on evidence generated by mixed methods studies. Pope et al. (2007) focus on three broad approaches to synthesizing evidence: (a) a quantitative approach where qualitative data, if included, are likely to be transformed into numbers to allow for statistical analysis; (b) interpretive qualitative approaches used to generate conceptual and theoretical understandings or explanations from a body of evidence; and (c) approaches drawing on diverse sources of evidence, both qualitative and quantitative. More recently, attention has been given to systematic reviews based primarily on qualitative research (Norris et al., 2010; Saini & Shlonsky, 2012).

This chapter contributes to an emerging dialog on reviews that include both qualitative and quantitative results. After additional background on review systems, the chapter outlines the opportunities and challenges of mixed methods reviews. We conclude with an argument for a more forward-thinking approach to assessing quality and synthesizing findings, an approach that includes increased attention to the ways in which qualitative and quantitative evidence is framed, depicted, and used in the evaluation(s) being reviewed.

The Structure of Systematic Reviews

The *systematic* in systematic reviews requires that the review be carried out to preagreed-upon standards. These include determining the question or questions to be addressed and the use of protocols for identifying relevant studies and appraising their quality, synthesizing findings, and updating the reviews (Nutley, Walter, & Davies, 2007). The questions may focus on the effectiveness of a specific intervention, as illustrated by SAMHSA's Registry of Evidence-Based Programs and Practices (http://www.nrepp.samhsa.gov/) or DOJ (Department of Justice) Model Programs Guide (http://www.ojjdp.gov/mpg/), or may compare the results of several similar interventions to learn about the conditions under which an approach may be successful, as found in AHRQ's EPCs or the Guide to Community Preventive Services (http://www.thecommunityguide.org).

Protocols for identifying relevant studies are driven by several factors, such as topic, population of interest, source (such as peer-reviewed journals), and time frame. Then, from the assembled literature, studies are screened in or out based on specified criteria, often related to study designs that are likely to provide credible evidence to address the review questions. Review protocols are then used to assess quality and focus on elements of study design and execution, data collection and analysis, and interpretation. Often, the protocols are available on the website associated with the review (e.g., http://crimesolutions.gov/about_instrument.aspx). In health care, at the request of Congress, the Institute of Medicine (IOM, 2011) developed standards for conducting systematic reviews of comparative effectiveness research. These standards are intended to inform public sponsors of systematic reviews. There is no counterpart to the IOM in the social and behavioral sciences; instead quality assessment is tailored by the review initiative and typically relies on generally accepted social science criteria for sound methodology.

As Cooksy and Caracelli (2009) point out, quality assessments in systematic reviews constitute a meta-evaluation step in the review process. Among various models for this step, two approaches predominate—independent reviews of evidence by researchers who assess the reliability of their assessments (e.g., Goldsmith, Bankhead, & Austoker, 2007), and an advisory panel model, where experts, following an initial review that culls the slate of interventions, determine whether particular interventions are supported by the most definitive evidence of effectiveness (e.g., Blueprints for Healthy Youth Development [http://www.blueprintsprogram.com]). Although systematic reviews have been touted as more defensible than traditional literature reviews, the methodology of a synthesis is vulnerable to bias at several points in the process, in particular, the inclusion/exclusion criteria and the quality review.

Design as a Selection Criterion in Review Systems

Just as evaluation designs are driven by the questions posed, so do the questions addressed by a systematic review drive the decision about what kind of studies to include. White and Waddington (2012), in a special issue on systematic reviews from an international development perspective, note that different questions require different approaches, and further that, to date, most completed systematic reviews have not drawn on the full range of available evidence. Snilstveit (2012) provides a formidable critique of systematic reviews, pointing out the narrow, increasingly criticized, focus of reviews relying on quantitative evidence to provide policy information on what works. Snilstveit points out the need for answers to a broader range of policy questions, the paucity of program theory, and limited reporting on implementation and context that can compromise both the construct and external validity of the review. To move beyond what Snilstveit refers to as bare-bones reviews, a theory-based, mixed methods systematic review is advocated. She offers two proposals: (a) make better use of data on the studies included in the review and (b) use additional sources of evidence such as process studies, project documents, and qualitative studies.

Systematic reviews that use multiple forms of evidence can be found mainly in the health arena to minimize the risk of overlooking adverse effects that could have dire consequences rather than expected beneficial treatment effects (Norris et al., 2010). Qualitative evidence in a systematic review can enhance an understanding of context, is an important asset in considering implementation fidelity, and may aid in explaining equivocal results or in determining how an intervention can be modified to strengthen its impact (Gibson & Duncan, 2005; Mihalic, 2004; Saini & Shlonsky, 2012). Norris et al. (2010) argue not only for the use of qualitative evidence in evaluation synthesis, but also for scholarship in modes of inquiry like mixed methods research to expand the frame of reference used to screen studies and examine study quality.

NEW DIRECTIONS FOR EVALUATION • DOI: 10.1002/ev

Both the Cochrane and Campbell Collaborations include methodological subgroups that are exploring how qualitative evidence might be taken into account. The Cochrane Handbook acknowledges that qualitative studies can play an important role in adding value to systematic reviews for policy, practice, and consumer decision making (Noyes, Popay, Pearson, Hannes, & Booth, 2008). One approach is to collect and analyze additional information on studies already included in the review when complementary studies or study components exist that shed light on findings. Another approach from the Cochrane review is to couple an effectiveness review with a linked review module that addresses additional questions, supplying a broader range of evidence (Snilstveit, 2012).

The Meta-Evaluative Step: Assessing Quality

A key step, and another potential source of bias, in systematic synthesis is the meta-evaluation—the evaluation of the quality—of the studies that have been selected. As mentioned earlier, the process usually involves either the independent review of studies by multiple researchers or a review by an advisory group. With the exception of the realist approach, which focuses mainly on testing underlying theories of change shared by different interventions (Pawson, 2006), most approaches rely on an appraisal checklist. Manning (2012) notes that although there is a proliferation of checklists, little work has been done to evaluate them. In mixed methods synthesis, one challenge with the use of checklists is how to operationalize quality criteria from different research traditions.

Although one can find many areas of overlap in the guidelines for assessing the quality of quantitative studies, common criteria for evaluating qualitative studies is more challenging because of the epistemological and ontological diversity of qualitative research and evaluation (Hannes & Lockwood, 2012). Some criteria from qualitative inquiry, such as those in Guba and Lincoln (1985)—credibility, transferability, dependability, and confirmability to establish the trustworthiness of findings—are well known and are considered analogs to more conventional validity criteria. However, it is recognized that qualitative evaluation "includes vastly different disciplinary, philosophical, theoretical, social and political commitments" (Sandelowski, Docherty, & Emden, 1997, p. 366).

To address the different foundations for qualitative research, Saini and Shlonsky (2012) developed a checklist intended to appraise studies in terms of epistemological and theoretical frameworks, ethical issues, and judgments about fairness and promotion of justice when the study focuses on empowering participants via participant-action research. They provide an overview for planning, developing, and implementing qualitative synthesis with the use of an approach that involves grouping studies with similar epistemological and ontological frameworks in order to promote philosophical consistency throughout the synthesis. Because the criteria for

New Directions for Evaluation • DOI: 10.1002/ev

judging evaluation quality reflect diverse conceptions of quality influenced by different paradigmatic stances and evaluands (Cooksy & Caracelli, 2009; Denzin, 2009), the primary concern in assessing qualitative evaluation has been the transparency of the qualitative process (Anfara, Brown, & Mangione, 2002; Jackson, 2010; Rudes, 2010).

As the field develops mixed methods synthesis of findings based on data collected from different epistemological and theoretical frameworks, the meta-evaluation aspect of the review becomes increasingly complex. Transparent criteria and methods are a necessary condition for being considered in evidence-based reviews whether in a qualitative synthesis or as part of expanding the frame of reference in evidence reviews emphasizing quantitative designs.

Movement Toward Mixed Methods Evidence-Based Reviews

Qualitative evidence synthesis methods have provided a segue for the consideration of mixed methods synthesis. At the primary study level, it is the mixed methods literature that addresses both qualitative and quantitative evidence and the purposes served by their inclusion in an evaluation. Evaluation scholars have considered the philosophical underpinnings and various types of mixed methods designs, as well as components of quality that enhance the practice of mixed methods studies evaluation and the quality of the inferences drawn from them (Greene & Caracelli, 1997; Greene, Caracelli, & Graham, 1989; Onwuegbuzie & Johnson, 2006; Teddlie & Tashakkori, 2003; and others). Onwuegbuzie and Johnson (2006), in discussing how to strengthen the validity of mixed methods studies, present the concept of legitimation in its various types as a dynamic, iterative process of evaluation that allows for substantiating inference quality. Greene (2007) notes that scholars in mixed methods, while still developing quality inquiry criteria, have come together in accepting method criteria to be guided by the method tradition of origin. However, with regard to criteria for warranting inferences from a mixed methods study, some blending or new creation may be needed. (For additional considerations on quality in mixed methods research, see Collins, Onwuegbuzie, & Jiao, 2006, 2007; Greene, 2007; Hesse-Biber, 2010; Pluye, Gagnon, Griffiths, & Johnson-Lafleur, 2009; Sandelowski, Voils, & Barroso, 2006; Teddlie & Tashakkori, 2009).

Pope et al. (2007) note that mixed methods studies have shown that both method genres have something to contribute at the primary level and that synthesis may be seen as a logical extension whereby both can make a contribution to understanding the processes that shape the implementation of programs. Among other authors, Saini and Shlonsky (2012) provide information on three approaches that have been used in some instances to combine quantitative and qualitative data at the level of synthesis: (a) Bayesian meta-analysis, which pools evidence from quantitative and qualitative studies with the use of statistical techniques (see Dixon-Woods,

Agarwal, Young, Jones, & Sutton, 2004); (b) realist synthesis, which takes into account the mechanisms (processes) and intervention outcomes based on multiple types of evidence (see Pawson, 2006); and (c) the Evidence for Policy and Practice Information and Co-ordinating Centre (EPPI-Centre), at the London Institute of Education, approach, which has developed methods for combining different types of evidence and yields two or more systematic syntheses to address different types of questions. The aim is to preserve the unique contributions of both method types, while also providing a way that each can contribute to the interpretation of the other, thus leading to more comprehensive and useful understanding of the main question of interest (Pope et al., 2007). Saini and Shlonsky point out that these three approaches are grounded in different epistemological frameworks and that epistemological and ontological positions remain an important part of the mixed methods discourse. Given the nascent stage of mixed methods inquiry, the authors urge caution when considering "the potent brew of mixed methods within systematic reviews" (p. 52).

Others advocate for developing mixed methods synthesis approaches as well, and some examples exist in practice (Harden & Thomas, 2005; Pope et al., 2007; Sandelowski et al., 2006). For example, Kavanagh, Campbell, Harden, and Thomas (2012) provide an illustration of a mixed methods synthesis approach developed by researchers at the EPPI-Centre. The synthesis was undertaken to review evidence of the effectiveness, acceptability, and feasibility of dietary and physical-activity interventions for weight management in pregnancy. There were three components to the synthesis. The first pertained to an effectiveness synthesis done according to established systematic review standards and used the Cochrane Collaboration's tool for assessing risk of bias. The second component was a qualitative synthesis to address questions related to effectiveness (intervention context, implementation, appropriateness, acceptability, and need). A "thematic synthesis" building on techniques from meta-ethnography (Noblit & Hare, 1988; Strauss & Corbin, 1998) was conducted with the use of generally interpretive findings or results with a primary focus on the views and experiences of participants. The studies were assessed for quality with the use of the tool for qualitative studies in the National Institute for Health and Clinical Excellence (NICE) Methods Manual (NICE, 2006). The tool draws on a range of qualitative checklists and covers such areas as theoretical approach, methods, context, rigor of analysis, richness of data, coherence of findings, and consideration of relevant ethical issues. The third component of the synthesis is the cross-study synthesis. It uses a conceptual and methodological matrix to juxtapose findings from the quantitative and qualitative syntheses. Then, through a comparative analysis, interventions that meet the needs and experiences of those targeted by the intervention or existing gaps in the primary intervention studies are identified. In this example, the views of pregnant women, their partners, families, and health professionals were juxtaposed with the content and findings of the interventions evaluated by the trials to help understand the mixed results of the outcome studies and inform recommendations for future research.

In the preceding example, the systematic reviews of qualitative and quantitative evidence are conducted separately. Both evidence types maintain their integrity, and through the cross-study synthesis both contribute to the systematic review findings. In another example, the actual studies that were synthesized already represent a combination of both method types. Heyvaert, Maes, and Onghena (2013) stress that although quality criteria have been identified for primary mixed methods studies, there is a gap concerning mixed methods studies for synthesis purposes. In a comprehensive mixed methods literature review, the authors develop a framework to perform mixed methods research synthesis (MMRS). The MMRS is described as a systematic review that applies principles of mixed methods research and takes into account data from qualitative, quantitative, and mixed primary-level studies. The authors summarize five dimensions applied to primary-level mixed methods design and select three—emphasis of approaches, temporal orientation, and integration—that they see as relevant at the synthesis level. By combining these dimensions they develop 18 MMRS designs and present two hypothetical examples to illustrate the approach.

Although the review was extensive, the primary mixed methods dimensions of purpose of study and theoretical framework are not in the MMRS framework. Heyvaert et al. (2013) acknowledge their importance but determine that differences among triangulation, explanatory, and exploratory purposes can be fit into their framework under emphasis of approach (equal status or one method type more dominant than the other), as well as their temporal orientation (simultaneous versus sequential use) of qualitative and quantitative approaches. However, by not considering a purpose such as triangulation the evaluator loses the quality intent to strengthen the inferences drawn from the study. Also, although there is discussion of the importance of integration at the synthesis level, it is not clear how integration, which has earned a discourse at the primary level of mixed methods studies, is taken into account. The complexity of the task is apparent for all engaged in understanding the burgeoning literature and how it affects practice. The authors readily acknowledge the paradigmatic assumptions that are debated in the primary mixed methods literature. Unfortunately, not taking theoretical framework into account at the synthesis level, or describing most mixed methods studies as pragmatic, does little to resolve these tensions that have implications for how we understand the quality of a study. The quality of the primary study is critical to the quality of the synthesis of studies.

Systematic reviews will always be reliant on primary studies. It is incumbent on such reviews to acknowledge their limitations and, by virtue of the information reviewed, to point out where primary research is needed.

Clarity by consensual understanding of what constitutes quality in primary research would appear to aid the meta-evaluative task of quality assessment in single studies and in a synthesis of studies. However, realistically, theorists and practitioners will bring different values and visions of what constitutes quality. There are multiple ways of knowing that characterize the evaluation field, and therefore the evaluation approaches used to resolve social problems will be characterized by a multiplicity of approaches (Greene, 2007). The language varies, yet in translation we may find a dynamic equivalence that allows for finding a common ground in judgments of study quality. That ground may mean that a diversity of views will be represented, including what they are able to bring or cannot bring to quality judgments. What is agreed upon is the need to use knowledge derived from qualitative and mixed methods studies to inform practice and policy.

With almost 20 years of continued research on research synthesis since the seminal *Handbook of Research Synthesis* was published, we find that the advice given by Cooper, Hedges and Valentine (1994) still holds. The knowledge gained from synthesis should have both intellectual quality and practical utility. Citing Wachter and Straf, who emphasized the importance of wisdom in research integration, they stress that wisdom starts with sound procedure. They add that structural integrity is only a minimal criterion for synthesis to lead to what we would call today, improving the general welfare or social betterment. A more general kind of design wisdom is also needed to build knowledge structures for such a purpose. In the ensuing years we have learned that design wisdom must include knowledge about context, culture, and values. Continued discourse about the quality of primary mixed methods studies is needed to support systematic reviews that provide more nuanced information about how interventions work and are responsive to a broad range of policy questions. It is the primary level of mixed methods research that holds the key to the best use of both qualitative and quantitative evidence in a systematic review.

References

Anfara, V. A., Jr., Brown, K. M., & Mangione, T. L. (2002). Qualitative analysis on stage: Making the research process more public. *Educational Researcher, 31*(7), 28–38.

Barnett-Page, E., & Thomas, J. (2009). Methods for the synthesis of qualitative research: A critical review (NCRM Working Paper Series, Number 01/09). Southampton, England: ESRC National Centre for Research Methods.

Caracelli, V. J. (2006). Enhancing the policy process through the use of ethnography and other study frameworks: A mixed methods strategy. *Research in the Schools, 13*(1), 84–92.

Collins, K. M. T., Onwuegbuzie, A. J., & Jiao, Q. G. (2006). Prevalence of mixed-methods sampling designs in social science research. *Evaluation & Research in Education, 19*, 83–101.

Collins, K. M. T., Onwuegbuzie, A. J., & Jiao, Q. G. (2007). A mixed methods investigation of mixed methods sampling designs in social and health science research. *Journal of Mixed Methods Research, 1*, 267–294.

Cooksy, L. J., & Caracelli, V. J. (2009). Meta-evaluation in practice: Selection and application of criteria. *Journal of Multidisciplinary Evaluation, 6*(11), 1–15.

Cooper, H., Hedges, L.V., & Valentine, J. C. (Eds.). (1994). *The handbook of research synthesis.* New York, NY: Russell Sage Foundation.

Denzin, N. K. (2009). The elephant in the living room: Or extending the conversation about the politics of evidence. *Qualitative Research, 9*(2), 139–160. doi:10.1177/1468794108098034

Dixon-Woods, M., Agarwal, S., Young, B., Jones, D., & Sutton, A. (2004). *Integrative approaches to qualitative and quantitative evidence.* London, England: Health Development Agency.

Gibson, C. M., & Duncan, G. J. (2005). Qualitative/quantitative synergies in a random-assignment program evaluation. In T. S. Weisner (Ed.), *Discovering successful pathways in children's development: Mixed methods in the study of childhood and family life* (pp. 283–303). Chicago, IL: University of Chicago Press.

Goldsmith, M. R., Bankhead, C. R., & Austoker, J. (2007). Synthesizing quantitative and qualitative research in evidence-based patient information. *Journal of Epidemiology and Community Health, 61*(3), 262–270. doi:10.1136/jech.2006.046110

Greene, J. C. (2007). *Mixed methods in social inquiry.* San Francisco, CA: Jossey-Bass.

Greene, J. C., & Caracelli, V. J. (Eds.). (1997). *Advances in mixed methods evaluation: The challenges and benefits of integrating diverse paradigms. New Directions for Evaluation, 74.*

Greene, J. C., Caracelli, V. J., & Graham, W. F. (1989). Toward a conceptual framework for mixed methods evaluation designs. *Educational Evaluation and Policy Analysis, 11*(3), 255–274.

Guba, E. G., & Lincoln, Y. S. (1985). *Naturalistic inquiry.* Beverly Hills, CA: Sage.

Hannes, K., & Lockwood, C. (Eds.). (2012). *Synthesizing qualitative research: Choosing the right approach.* West Sussex, United Kingdom: Wiley-Blackwell.

Hansen, H. F., & Rieper, O. (2009). The evidence movement: The development and consequences of methodologies in review practices. *Evaluation, 15,* 141–163. doi:10.1177/1356389008101968

Harden, A., & Thomas, J. (2005). Methodological issues in combining diverse study types in systematic reviews. *International Journal of Social Research Methodology, 8*(3), 257–271.

Hesse-Biber, S. N. (2010). *Mixed methods research: Merging theory with practice.* New York: NY: The Guilford Press.

Heyvaert, M., Maes, B., & Onghena, P. (2013). Mixed methods research synthesis: Definition, framework, and potential. *Quality & Quantity, 47,* 659–676. doi:10.1007/s11135-011-9538-6

Institute of Medicine. (2011). *Finding what works in health care. Standards for systematic reviews.* Washington, DC: The National Academies Press.

Jackson, K. (July, 2010). *"Transparency" in different communities of practice.* 6th Mixed Methods International Conference, Baltimore, MD.

Kavanagh, J., Campbell, F., Harden, A., & Thomas, J. (2012). Mixed methods synthesis: A worked example. In K. Hannes & C. Lockwood (Eds.), *Synthesizing qualitative research: Choosing the right approach* (pp. 113–136). West Sussex, United Kingdom: Wiley-Blackwell.

Labin, S. (2008). Research synthesis: Toward broad-based evidence. In N. L. Smith & P. R. Brandon (Eds.), *Fundamental issues in evaluation* (89–110). New York, NY: Guilford.

Manning, N. (2012). Conclusion. In K. Hannes & C. Lockwood (Eds.), *Synthesizing qualitative research: Choosing the right approach.* West Sussex, United Kingdom: Wiley-Blackwell.

Mihalic, S. (2004). The importance of implementation fidelity. *Emotional & Behavioral Disorders in Youth, 4*(4), 81–109.

National Institute for Health and Clinical Excellence. (2006). *Public health guidance: Development process and methods.* London, England: National Institute for Health and Clinical Excellence.

Noblit, G. W., & Hare, R. D. (1988). *Meta-ethnography: Synthesizing qualitative studies.* Newbury Park, CA: Sage.

Norris, S., Atkins, D., Bruening, W., Fox, S., Johnson, E., Kane, R., . . . Viswanathan, M. (2010). Selecting observational studies for comparing medical interventions. In *Methods guide for comparative effectiveness reviews.* Rockville, MD: Agency for Healthcare Research and Quality. Retrieved from http://www.effectivehealthcare.ahrq.gov/ehc/products/196/454/MethodsGuideNorris_06042010.pdf

Noyes, J., Popay, J., Pearson, A., Hannes, K., & Booth, A. (2008). Chapter 20: Qualitative research and Cochrane reviews. In J. P. T. Higgins & S. Green (Eds.), *Cochrane handbook for systematic reviews of interventions.* Version 5.0.1 [updated September 2008]. The Cochrane Collaboration, 2008. Retrieved from http://www.igh.org/Cochrane/tools/Ch20_Qualitative.pdf

Nutley, S. M., Walter, I., & Davies, H. T. O. (2007). *Using evidence: How research can inform public services.* Chicago, IL: University of Chicago Press.

Onwuegbuzie, A. J., & Johnson, R. B. (2006). The validity issue in mixed research. *Research in the Schools, 13,* 48–63.

Pawson, R. (2006). *Evidence-based policy: A realist perspective.* Thousand Oaks, CA: Sage.

Pluye, P., Gagnon, M.-P., Griffiths, F., & Johnson-Lafleur, J. (2009). A scoring system for appraising mixed methods research, and concomitantly appraising qualitative, quantitative and mixed methods primary studies in mixed studies reviews. *International Journal of Nursing Studies, 46,* 529–546.

Pope, C., Mays, N., & Popay, J. (2007). *Synthesizing qualitative and quantitative research: A guide to methods.* Berkshire, England: Open University Press.

Rossi, P. H., Lipsey, M. W., & Freeman, H. E. (2004). *Evaluation* (7th ed.). Thousand Oaks, CA: Sage.

Rudes, D. S. (2010, April). *Qualitative fieldwork contributions to the study of evidence-based practices.* Presented at the 10th Annual Jerry Lee Crime Prevention Symposium, University of Maryland, College Park, MD.

Saini, M., & Shlonsky, A. (2012). *Systematic synthesis of qualitative research.* Oxford, England: Oxford University Press.

Sandelowski, M., Docherty, S., & Emden, C. (1997). Qualitative metasynthesis: Issues and techniques. *Research in Nursing & Health, 20,* 365–371.

Sandelowski, M., Voils, C. I., & Barroso, J. (2006). Defining and designing mixed research synthesis studies. *Research in the Schools, 13*(1), 29–40.

Snilstveit, B. (2012). Systematic reviews: From "bare bones" reviews to policy relevance. *Journal of Development Effectiveness, 4*(3), 388–408.

Strauss, A. L., & Corbin, J. (1998). *Basics of qualitative research: Techniques and procedures for developing grounded theory.* Thousand Oaks, CA: Sage.

Teddlie, C., & Tashakkori, A. (2003). Major issues and controversies in the use of mixed methods in the social and behavioral sciences. In A. Tashakkori & C. Teddlie (Eds.), *Handbook of mixed methods in social and behavioral research* (pp. 3–50). Thousand Oaks, CA: Sage.

Teddlie, C., & Tashakkori, A. (2009). *Foundations of mixed methods research: Integrating quantitative and qualitative techniques in the social and behavioral sciences.* Thousand Oaks, CA: Sage.

U.S. Government Accountability Office. (1992a). *Cross design synthesis: A new strategy for medical effectiveness research* (GAO-92–18). Retrieved from http://www.gao.gov/products/PEMD-92–18

U.S. Government Accountability Office. (1992b). *The evaluation synthesis* (PEMD-10.1.2). Retrieved from http://gao.gov/products/PEMD-10.1.2

U.S. Government Accountability Office. (2003). *Ethnographic studies can inform agencies' actions* (GAO-03-455). Retrieved from http://www.gao.gov/products/GAO-03-455

U.S. Government Accountability Office. (2009). *Program evaluation: A variety of rigorous methods can help identify effective interventions* (GAO-10-30). Retrieved from http://www.gao.gov/products/GAO-10-30

U.S. Government Accountability Office. (2012). *President's emergency plan for AIDS relief: Agencies can enhance evaluation quality, planning, and dissemination* (GAO-12-673). Retrieved from http://www.gao.gov/products/GAO-12-673

White, H., & Waddington, H. (2012). Why do we care about evidence synthesis? An introduction to the special issue on systematic reviews. *Journal of Development Effectiveness, 4*(3), 351–358.

Zief, S., & Agodini, R. (2012). *Supporting policy and program decisions: Recommendations for conducting high quality systematic evidence reviews.* Center for Improving Research Evidence Issue Brief. Retrieved from http://www.mathematica-mpr.com/publications/PDFs/education/systematic_reviews_ib.pdf

VALERIE J. CARACELLI is senior social science analyst at the U.S. Government Accountability Office. She served on the AEA Board (2007–2009) and currently serves on the board of the Washington Evaluators.

LESLIE J. COOKSY is director of evaluation at the Sierra Health Foundation in Sacramento. She was 2010 President of the American Evaluation Association.

New Directions for Evaluation • DOI: 10.1002/ev

10

Reflections and Ruminations

Jennifer C. Greene

Abstract

*This is a timely issue on the contributions of mixed methodology to the contem-
porary demand for credible evaluative evidence on which to base policy and
resource-allocation decisions. The character of evidence—especially evidence
on the quality and effectiveness of efforts to improve the life quality or even life
chances of many in our societies—requires the best minds from all corners of
the evaluation community. The mixed methods voice is needed in the evidence-
based conversation.* ©Wiley Periodicals, Inc., and the American Evaluation
Association.

This issue offers a kaleidoscope of perspectives on the contributions
of a mixed methods approach to the credibility of evidence generated in evaluation studies. The metaphor of a kaleidoscope is apt, as
this issue is designed to engage the complex intersections of three distinct
social scientific frames:

1. The *context* for the issue is the social practice of evaluation.
2. The *methodology* being engaged is the emerging field of mixing methods in social inquiry.
3. The *issue or challenge* being addressed is the contemporary and contested discourse about the meanings and relevance of credible evidence
   in evaluation contexts.

NEW DIRECTIONS FOR EVALUATION, no. 138, Summer 2013 © Wiley Periodicals, Inc., and the American Evaluation
Association. Published online in Wiley Online Library (wileyonlinelibrary.com) • DOI: 10.1002/ev.20062

The issue's authors differentially emphasize these three frames, generating varied patterns of meaning as the kaleidoscope rotates through the chapters. The kaleidoscope metaphor is further relevant because the issue is explicitly designed by the editors to examine the contributions of mixed methods evaluation and its emerging philosophies, theories, and practices to the credibility of evaluation findings. So the varied patterns of discussion and meaning in the chapters are also created by the chapters' differential focus on mixed methods philosophical stances, theoretical perspectives, and/or practical strategies, respectively.

In this commentary, I first describe the chapters with the use of the kaleidoscopic dimensions introduced above. These descriptions include the authors' ideas about the meanings of credible evidence in the context of their chapters, as stated or, in some cases, as inferred by me. I then consider the following questions, and endeavor to synthesize this issue's contributions to them.

How is *credible evaluative evidence* conceptualized from a mixed methods perspective?

What are the promises and potentials of generating credible evidence from a mixed methods approach to evaluation? What about the practice of mixing methods underlies such promises?

How well does a mixed methods approach to evaluation fulfill such promises at present? What else is needed?

Spinning the Kaleidoscope

I have sorted the preceding nine chapters of this issue into the following clusters. In Cluster One are the first four chapters, all of which focus on the paradigmatic and philosophical dimensions of mixed methodology. Cluster Two includes the issue's next three chapters, which can be roughly categorized as articles that theorize about mixed—or multiple—methodology, and illustrate this theorizing with evaluation examples. And Cluster Three features the final two chapters that focus on two facets of mixed methods practice, specifically, developing sampling strategies and conducting mixed methods effectiveness reviews of evaluation studies.

Cluster One—Pondering Paradigms

The introductory chapter by the editors provides an overview of the mixed methods field and then concentrates on the paradigmatic or philosophical strands of the mixed methods conversation. The next three chapters, by design, also concentrate on philosophical issues. Jori N. Hall presents Deweyan pragmatism as a practical philosophical framework for mixed methods evaluation, and draws implications for a pragmatic view of credible evidence. Donna Mertens offers the major assumptions of the transformative paradigm for evaluation. And R. Burke Johnson and Tres Stefurak introduce their process-oriented paradigm of dialectical pluralism for evaluation.

I enthusiastically applaud this emphasis on paradigms and philosophy, especially in an issue on mixed methods evaluation, for three main reasons. (See also Denscombe, 2008.) First, a continuing and critical issue in the mixed methods discussion is indeed the plausibility and defensibility of mixing at the *paradigmatic level*, in addition to the level of *method* (interview, questionnaire) and *methodology* (case study, survey, experiment) (Greene, 2007; Teddlie & Tashakkori, 2010). This issue can be labeled as one's stance on mixing paradigms while mixing methods, or one's "paradigm stance" (Greene, 2007). I suggest that there are four primary paradigm stances regarding the mixing of paradigms in mixed methods inquiry:

1. A *complementary-strengths* stance welcomes multiple paradigms while maintaining the integrity of each by not mixing until the end of the study.
2. A *dialectic* stance welcomes multiple paradigms (not just postpositivism and constructivism), along with ongoing conversation and interaction among them.
3. An *a-paradigmatic* stance privileges the inputs of substantive theory and context over philosophy in making important practice decisions.
4. An *alternative paradigm* stance welcomes other paradigmatic viewpoints as guides for mixed methods inquiry, notably pragmatism and transformation, which have now become part of the mixed methods conversation.

Further, I argue that careful explication of just what is being mixed in a mixed methods study contributes to the subsequent warrant for and thus credibility of results. As the present issue illustrates, diverse standpoints on this issue persist, and I believe that it well behooves the mixed methods community to keep this conversation respectfully open and lively.

Second, in this era of paradigm pluralism, it is quite important for mixed methods inquirers (and, in fact, all other social inquirers) to be explicit about the paradigmatic assumptions that frame and guide their work. All social science is framed and guided by inquirer assumptions about the nature of the social world, about what counts as warranted knowledge, about defensible methodology, and about the role of social inquiry in society, among others. It is simply not possible to conduct social inquiry without a self-understanding of the purpose and character of this activity (Schwandt, 2002). Third, it is a critical responsibility of the *inquirer* to make these assumptions explicit *and* to justify the values they invoke—values of distance, engagement, inclusion, objectivity, generalizability, contextuality, social action, and so forth. This is particularly important in evaluation contexts, because they are saturated with values. Absent this information, warrants for the credibility of evaluative findings are reduced and misinterpretations more likely. So, I strongly endorse this emphasis on philosophical paradigms in this issue on mixed methods' contributions to credible evaluation processes and results.

Like a kaleidoscope, the authors in this issue have engaged in various ways with the paradigm challenges of mixed methods approaches to evaluation and with their implications for the credibility of the evaluative evidence attained. Following their issue overview, the editors concentrate in the first chapter on introducing additional paradigm standpoints, "seek[ing] to remap and reshape the paradigmatic landscape, often to address the thorny paradigmatic issues involved in the mixing of methods and methodologies within a single evaluation project" (p. 10). Four additional paradigm standpoints are recommended in particular for mixed methods inquiry (research and evaluation), each of which is engaged in subsequent chapters—American pragmatism (Chapter 2), transformation (Chapter 3), dialectical pluralism (Chapter 4), and pluralism (Chapter 7). While not favoring any particular paradigm in this introduction, Mertens and Hesse-Biber suggest that careful and explicit attention to paradigmatic assumptions, along with the inclusion of multiple paradigmatic stances and viewpoints in mixed methods evaluation, contribute to the credibility of evidence thus obtained.

In Chapter 2, Jori N. Hall offers a scholarly discussion of the character of Deweyan pragmatism and its applicability to mixed methods evaluation and to debates about the character of credible evidence. Echoing other critics of an instrumental or "what works" understanding of pragmatism, Hall thoughtfully engages the philosophical cornerstones of Dewey's pragmatism. These include an ontological stance of "transactional realism, which moves away from the traditional dualism of objectivity and subjectivity" (p. 17), in favor of a view of knowledge as both constructed and real, as "temporal and embedded in and generated through our experiential transactions" (p. 17). Further, "truth is linked to action" (p. 17), especially "intelligent action." Intelligent action generates warranted assertions through problem identification and analysis, an ethical stance of considering seriously the perspectives of others, and a valuing of communities as social spaces for actions that advance democratic ideals in society. Hall concludes that the idea of credible evidence is best reflected in Dewey's core construct of warranted assertions, which includes the quality of the means or methods, as well as "continuous reflections on evaluation practices [the means] and the consequences they have in the lives of people" (p. 21), consequences that centrally engage "the extent to which evaluative endeavors promote values of democracy" (p. 24).

In Chapter 3, Donna Mertens presents the core assumptions of the transformative paradigm for social inquiry, along with illustrations from evaluation contexts. In this alternative-paradigm mixed methods stance, the core assumptions all engage values and issues of justice. In this way, political and values considerations related to the well-being of marginalized peoples trump more abstract, decontextualized considerations of philosophy and method. That is, the purpose, audience, and design of a transformative evaluation study are shaped most importantly by values assumptions and action agendas, rather than by more rarefied philosophical tenets or methodological principles. So, although a mixed methods approach often works effectively in service of transformative commitments, this alternative paradigm is not inherently linked to mixing methods. From Mertens' transformative lens, credible evaluative evidence foregrounds the cultural, economic, and contextual perspectives and experiences of the community members the program is intended to serve and embodies commitments to social justice and social action.

The final chapter that I allocated to the philosophy and paradigm section presents dialectical pluralism, "a *process* philosophy for dialoging with difference" (Johnson & Stefurak, p. 38, emphasis in original). The authors of this chapter advocate for including and engaging with multiple and diverse stakeholder standpoints in evaluation, and for embracing Rawlsian commitments to procedural justice. A stance of dialectical pluralism respects and invites dialogue among values representing the conceptual and the practical, the societal and the local, the utilitarian and the justice-oriented. The authors argue that this is best accomplished via a mixed methods approach, which generates results constructed from multiple standpoints, beliefs, and values, each respected and each dialogically engaged. So, from a stance of dialectical pluralism, an evaluation conducted with these dialogic processes and values commitments to justice would generate meaningful, useful, and also credible evaluative evidence.

In sum, the considerable space allocated in this issue to paradigms, philosophical assumptions, and their associated value commitments underscores the central role these all play in arguments about credible evidence—even though those arguments rarely engage the assumptive domains of philosophy or values. So, one important contribution of this issue is to remind us that *credible evidence* is a construct, shaped differently by different assumptions about social reality, social knowledge, the presence and character of values in empirical inquiry, and the political context of the discourse. A second important contribution of this issue is these authors' quiet insistence on an inclusive, reflective, actionable, democratic, transformative view of credible evidence in evaluation contexts—one that intentionally and respectfully attends to the experiences and standpoints of multiple and diverse evaluation stakeholders. Further, such meaningful engagement with and inclusion of the rich diversity of experience and standpoint presented by evaluation contexts is often best accomplished via a mixed methods evaluation approach—an argument offered by these chapter authors and echoed by this author.

Cluster Two—Tapping Into Theory

The kaleidoscope now spins to mixed-methods theory and selected theorizing. Chapter 5 by Sharlene Hesse-Biber and Chapter 6 by Howard White both engage the contributions of a mixed methods perspective to the information and inferences obtained about program impacts from a randomized controlled experiment, albeit in quite different ways. In Chapter 7, Nollaig Frost and Sevasti-Melissa Nolas argue for the use of multiple qualitative methods, or a multimethod approach in evaluation studies.

Both Hesse-Biber and White anchor their discussions in randomized controlled (experimental) trials (RCTs) because much of the contemporary discourse elevates this particular methodology as the gold standard in generating credible evaluative evidence about program impacts or outcomes. In this method-driven discourse, evidence about *intended* program outcomes or impacts is most highly valued, yet this emphasis is rarely explicitly defended. Hesse-Biber and White each argue for an *expansion* of the kinds of evidence generated in evaluation, as ways (a) to extend the reach of the evaluation to other important features of the program and its context, beyond data on the magnitude of outcomes, and (b) to strengthen the warrants for the outcome information obtained.

Hesse-Biber specifically argues for the addition of subjectivist qualitative methods at various points in an RCT (before, during, and after) in order to represent the perspectives and experiences of the program beneficiaries and staff better, as well as to monitor the quality of the experimental protocols. For example, qualitative data collected from prospective participants and staff *prior to* the experiment could enhance recruitment quality, as well as assess the meanings of program success from these stakeholder perspectives.

White offers a parallel argument in which he shifts the focus from mixing methods to engaging both counterfactual and factual analyses. The point is not to mix methods, he argues, but rather to extend the reach of the study to questions beyond impact. Specifically, "RCTs should be embedded in a broader evaluation design, which combines the counterfactual analysis of attribution with a factual analysis across the causal chain," the latter referring to an assessment of the underlying program theory (p. 62). With sufficient samples, quantitative experimental designs are best for counterfactual analysis, whereas both quantitative and qualitative methods are useful for factual analysis. White supports his core argument with lively examples from the field. These examples emphasize the contributions of grounded qualitative data to understand context, design a questionnaire, assess fidelity of implementation, distinguish between theory failure and implementation failure, and understand causal mechanisms of change, among other possibilities. Unlike Hesse-Biber, White's argument for mixing does not encompass the paradigmatic level, but rather remains at the levels of method and methodology.

NEW DIRECTIONS FOR EVALUATION • DOI: 10.1002/ev

These arguments echo the early impetus for mixing methods in evaluation—to expand the reach of the study to multiple program components, to diverse perspectives, and to the program as both designed and experienced—a purpose for mixing currently called *expansion*. The arguments do not directly challenge the status quo of impact evaluations (the RCT as the gold standard), but rather seek to enhance it. (A mixed methods perspective *does* offer the potential for a significant challenge to the RCT as the gold standard for generation of credible evidence.) Like the examples provided by both authors, in expansion designs the methods often assess different constructs and remain separate throughout the study. A mixed methods expansion design, that is, expands the questions, data, and results obtained from an otherwise more limited study. By inference, these authors appear to be arguing for a reconceptualization of credibility in impact evaluations that is also substantially expanded—from aggregate data on outcomes attained to data also on program design, causal logic, implementation, and experience, needed, for example, to interpret the outcome data better and for external validity. By inference, credibility in impact evaluation for these authors is a multidimensional construct inclusive of a complex and contextual program portrait. Credibility is issue driven, not method driven.

The final chapter in this cluster on theorizing about mixed methods is actually about qualitatively driven multiple methods. In this chapter, Frost and Nolas argue that "pluralistic qualitative research" is most appropriate for evaluations of innovative, small-scale interventions, about which data on processes and "proof of concept" (of the underlying program theory) are as important as data on outcomes, especially for audiences other than policy makers. This chapter addresses contexts where the program is still in development, rather than contexts where "proud programs" (Campbell, 1998) are ready for outcome evaluation. In these and other ways, the chapter is reminiscent of the ascendance of qualitative methodologies in applied social science several decades ago. Although I believe there are important distinctions between mixed and multiple methods approaches, the heart of the Frost and Nolas argument parallels the core argument for mixing methods—that the use of a plurality of methods engages a diversity of standpoints, which in turn yields richer, deeper, and better understanding of key evaluation constructs and phenomena. However, the connections to the meanings of credible evidence in evaluation contexts, especially evaluations of outcomes, are underdeveloped.

In summary, all of these authors clearly suggest that evaluative results are enhanced when they represent multiple facets of a program as designed, implemented, and experienced; multiple standpoints on what is valued about a program; and multiple ideals and aspirations for a social intervention. One can surmise that this valuing of multiplicity, expansiveness, and pluralism extends to the concept of credible evaluative evidence.

Cluster Three—Perspectives on Practice

The final two chapters of this issue engage two issues of mixed methods evaluation practice. Kathleen Collins and Tony Onwuegbuzie discuss mixed methods sampling strategies. Valerie Caracelli and Leslie Cooksy offer insights into systematic reviews that aim to assess the credibility of extant evidence on a particular intervention or practice. They further offer commentary on the current state of mixed methods evidence-based practice reviews.

Collins and Onwuegbuzie argue that sampling decisions are related to the subsequent quality and thus credibility of inferences. They then concentrate their discussion on the mixed methods methodological quality criterion of interpretive consistency, which they define as the "consistency between the [mixed methods] sampling designs and the conclusions, inferences, generalizations, and transferability of findings" (p. 86). Clearly, methodological quality *is* related to the credibility of evidence in evaluation. In fact, much of the contemporary debate about credible evidence is actually anchored in—and thus constitutes debate about—different conceptualizations of what constitutes methodological quality. These authors maintain a focus on methodological quality as the primary condition for credibility of evidence in social inquiry, and do so by offering a framework of quality parameters in mixed methods sampling.

Caracelli and Cooksy present a comprehensive portrait of the state of the art of systematic reviews regarding the status of credible evidence on a particular intervention or practice. Echoing Hesse-Biber and White, they observe that *primary* mixed methods evaluation studies can offer information not just on outcome attainment, but also on context, process, and implementation fidelity, as well as explanatory insights into underlying mechanisms of change; and they further argue that such enhanced information contributes to enhanced credibility. In parallel, mixed methods synthesis *reviews*, or reviews of a mixed set of evaluations (realist, constructivist, and mixed methods), can also offer enhanced credibility of the resulting evidence. These authors highlight the progress made toward a process for mixed methods reviews and provide rich illustrations of milestones marking this progress. Further, the authors thoughtfully discuss the continuing challenges mixed methods reviews encounter, notably challenges of differing paradigmatic assumptions and, concomitantly, differing criteria for judging methodological quality. The latter (methodological quality) is a cornerstone of credibility, but, as the authors in this chapter—and in this issue more broadly—suggest, is insufficient all by itself.

Mixed Methods and Credible Evidence in Evaluation

The dominant political discourse of today equates credibility of evaluative evidence with strong methodology of a particular sort, namely, the randomized controlled experiment. Well-done experiments, argue proponents, can yield sound evidence on the attainment of the *intended outcomes* of social, educational, and health programs. Often muted in this discourse are the justifications for privileging intended outcomes in studies of such interventions, along with privileging decision and policy makers as the primary audiences for evaluation studies. Similarly muted are the justifications for narrowing not just the methodology, but also the paradigmatic assumptions, worldviews, and value stances that frame evidence-based evaluation to just one set—those of postpositivism. These notably include the assumptions of realism and the value stances of objectivity, generalizability, instrumentality, efficiency, and effectiveness.

When applied to the challenges of generating credible evidence for decision making, the methodologically self-conscious domain of mixing methods rather quickly exposes these muted dimensions of the contemporary conversation about credible evidence and holds them up for scrutiny. This is because the very concept of mixing methods inherently invokes a dialogic engagement (Greene, 2007) with one or more strands of difference, strands that comprise the multidimensional fabric of diverse social science methodologies. In some ways, this may be the most valuable contribution of mixed methodology to the generation of credible evidence in evaluation. Credibility is not simply methodologically granted by the use of an RCT, but rather must be earned by dialogic means and argument beyond methodology (Greene, 2012).

The authors in this issue take some important steps toward a full-fledged mixed methods vision of the character of credible evidence in evaluation contexts. The first set of chapters foregrounds the defining role played by often-unstated paradigmatic assumptions and values in what constitutes credible evidence. These discussions further argue for the importance of multiplicity and pluralism via the inclusion of diverse stakeholder experiences, standpoints, and values in what counts as credible evaluative evidence. Evaluation is a social practice with multiple legitimate stakeholders, interests, and claims on resources. Credibility in evaluation therefore must encompass some plurality of such perspectives and interests. Some authors in the first set of chapters further suggest that credible evidence in evaluation is *actionable*. This connects directly with the evaluation field's premium on being of use, on providing useful information of meaningful consequence to stakeholders in the contexts being studied. This distinctive utilization-oriented character of evaluation is importantly part of any portrait of credible evaluative evidence.

The second set of chapters in this issue emphasize the mixed methods theoretical concept of *expansion*, by which the breadth and depth of an evaluation study is increased and enhanced through the use of more than one method, methodology, and/or paradigmatic framework. In particular, an impact/outcome evaluation can be, and perhaps should be, augmented via qualitative methods that offer useful and important information on program experiences, implementation, context, and components of program theory. By implication, evidence on outcomes alone, or evidence from black-box evaluations, is not sufficient for credibility from a mixed methods perspective. Also needed is information that contextualizes such evidence and offers insights into program implementation and the warrants for the underlying program theory (what Howard White calls "causal chain analysis").

Further development of this line of theorizing with other mixed methods purposes, designs, and analysis strategies will be very fruitful. For example, in addition to expansion, purposes for mixed methods evaluations include initiation and triangulation. Initiation values divergence and the additional novel insights that it may bring, and triangulation values convergence and the additional confidence in results obtained that it affords. How might each of these mixed methods purposes and designs contribute to the credibility of evaluative evidence?

Glimpses of mixed methods practice and its connections to credible evidence are offered in the third set of chapters in this issue, including the highly relevant chapter on mixed methods synthesis reviews. It is evident—from journal and conference submissions, methodology courses, listserves, and more—that mixed methods practice has exploded over the past decade. It is equally evident that there remains a considerable gap between mixed methods theory and mixed methods practice. Many empirical researchers and evaluators who use a mixed methods approach do so with little cognizance of the breadth and depth of mixed methods theory and thus the potential of this methodology to contribute to credible evidence about consequential solutions to the world's pressing problems. Closer conversations between mixed methods theory and practice can help close this gap.

Reprise

This issue constructively engages the methodological dimensions of the contemporary conversation about the nature of credible evidence in evaluation practice. Specifically, this issue offers a mixed methods perspective on this conversation and includes paradigmatic, theoretical, and practical dimensions of what the mixed methods field can offer to credibility of evidence in evaluation contexts. As a strong proponent of mixing methods in evaluation, I applaud the contributions of the authors and editors of this issue. At the same time, I believe it is important to recall the importance of the *relational* facets of evaluation as a social practice (Abma, 2006; Greene, DeStefano, Burgon, & Hall, 2006). Methodology, even of the mixed genre, will ever need the assistance of relationships in the contexts at hand for full enactment of the promises of credibility.

References

Abma, T. A. (2006). The social relations of evaluation. In I. F. Shaw, J. C. Greene, & M. M. Mark (Eds.), *The Sage handbook of evaluation* (pp. 184–199). London, England: Sage.

Campbell, D. T. (1998). The experimenting society. In W. N. Dunn (Ed.), *The experimenting society: Essays in honor of Donald T. Campbell, Policy Studies Review Annual, Volume 11* (pp. 35–68). Piscataway, NJ: Transaction Publishers.

Denscombe, M. (2008). Communities of practice: A research paradigm for the mixed methods approach. *Journal of Mixed Methods Research, 2*(3), 270–283.

Greene, J. C. (2007). *Mixed methods in social inquiry.* San Francisco, CA: Wiley.

Greene, J. C. (2012). Las contribution des données probantes au processus de crédibilisation d'une évaluation [How evidence earns credibility in evaluation]. In M. Hurteau, S. Houle & F. Guillemette (Eds.), *L'évaluation de programme axée sur le jugement crédible* (pp. 57–73). Québec, Canada: Les Presses de l'Université du Québec.

Greene, J. C., DeStefano, L., Burgon, H., & Hall, J. (2006). An educative, values-engaged approach to evaluating STEM educational programs. In D. Huffman & F. Lawrenz (Eds.), *Critical issues in STEM evaluation. New Directions for Evaluation, 109,* 53–71.

Schwandt, T. A. (2002). *Evaluation practice reconsidered.* Oxford, England: Peter Lang.

Teddlie, C., & Tashakkori, A. (2010). Overview of contemporary issues in mixed methods research. In A. Tashakkori & C. Teddlie (Eds.), *Sage handbook of mixed methods in social and behavioral research* (pp. 1–44). Thousand Oaks, CA: Sage.

JENNIFER C. GREENE *is a professor of educational psychology at the University of Illinois at Urbana-Champaign.*

NEW DIRECTIONS FOR EVALUATION • DOI: 10.1002/ev

INDEX